THE POWER OF THE PATCH

For this reason I say to you, do not be worried about your life, as to what you will eat or what you will drink; nor for your body, as to what you will put on. Is life not more than food, and the body more than clothing? Look at the birds of the sky, that they do not sow, nor reap, nor gather crops into barns, and yet your heavenly Father feeds them. Are you not much more important than they? And which of you by worrying can add a single day to his life's span? And why are you worried about clothing? Notice how the lilies of the field grow; they do not labor nor do they spin thread for cloth, yet I say to you that not even Solomon in all his glory clothed himself like one of these. But if God so clothes the grass of the field, which is alive today and tomorrow is thrown into the furnace, will He not much more clothe you? You of little faith! Do not worry then, saying, 'What are we to eat?' or 'What are we to drink?' or 'What are we to wear for clothing?' For the Gentiles eagerly seek all these things; for your heavenly Father knows that you need all these things. But seek first His kingdom and His righteousness, and all these things will be provided to you.

So do not worry about tomorrow; for tomorrow will worry about itself. Each day has enough trouble of its own.

~Matthew 6:25–34

THE
POWER
OF THE
PATCH

GREG VANDAGRIFF

WordCrafts Press

The Power of the Patch
Copyright © 2025
Greg Vandagriff

Hardback ISBN: 978-1-962218-92-4
Paperback ISBN: 978-1-962218-93-1

Published by WordCrafts Press
Cody, Wyoming 82414
www.wordcrafts.net

Contents

To all of those men that feel ill equipped, unprepared and not ready to be a Dad, let alone a Dad Legend. You can do it! One day at a time.

Pre-Game

Hello. I want to take a moment to set the stage for this book. Currently (in the year 2024), I am finishing my 35th year as a high school football coach. One of the best things we do in our program is the Father/Son Dinner we host near the end of each football season. The entire football team, coaches, and support personnel attend the function. But the seniors and their dads are the ones we're honoring. We serve them steaks and everyone else gets hamburgers and hot dogs. If a student-athlete makes it all the way through our program, his dad (or important, male, role model) gets to come share this senior year honor.

When the dads arrive at the dinner, I hand them a sheet of paper with three questions on it. They are to answer these easy questions about their sons in front of the entire team. Many of the dads immediately begin to sweat and get anxious about having to do this . . . and I want them to be uncomfortable. Also, several dads ask, "Why didn't you give this to me yesterday, so that I could've had time to think about it?" Well, that is exactly the point. I do not want them to have more than fifteen minutes to think about these extremely basic questions. I know what you are thinking: "What are the questions?" Well, I am not going to let that out of the bag. They're not complex questions, but they are definitely from the heart. I need every dad to feel some emotion as they answer. The players answer the same basic questions about their dads.

Once the seniors and their dads have had time to complete the questions and eat, the program begins. I stand up front and talk about the fact that I never experienced something like this with my dad and how special this moment can be. If each dad and son are authentic and forget there is anyone else in the room, they can create a moment for each other that neither will ever forget. It is in these moments that, through the tears, I have watched the dads and players share their hearts about one another. It was in moments like this that I began to realize what I needed to do—start a crusade to help dads be a stronger part of their children's lives. I also realized that if it were not for solid coaches and men in my life, I would have been clueless about being a strong dad. So, if I can help motivate other dads to have stronger roles in their kids' lives, they too can begin to heal the unhealthiness that may exist in their family trees, as I have.

My Why

I've wanted to write this book for many years. I had no idea who would desire to read it, but I knew I could not be the only man in the world who felt so ill-prepared and completely unqualified to be a good dad. When you grow up without the example of a good dad, how do you become one? Thus begin the questions that enter your mind once you begin having your own children. When my wife, Kelly, and I were preparing for our first child, I was bombarded with emotions. I couldn't believe I was getting the chance to be a dad. It was real! But then came the overwhelming emotions of how unprepared I was for this challenge.

I'm writing this book to share not only the failures and the sense of inadequacy I had in my own life but also the undeniable reality that we (men) are the reason our country (and the world) is in the situation it's in right now. It's largely due to our desire to be self-fulfilled instead of being willing and ready to take on the responsibility of being a role model to our own children. Statistically, it's overwhelming how destructive it is for the life of a child when the dad is not present in the home.

Now, it's one thing to be a physical body within the home but it's another thing to be an active participant in the raising of your children—to be a consistent source of healthy discipline and love for them. If sharing my experiences can help even one Dad become more equipped to step up to the plate, it's more than worth it. As you read through the stories in this book, and the lessons they taught me, maybe you will be prompted to think of some of your own stories. Maybe you will learn fresh lessons from experiences in which you survived or thrived. Many of the stories I'll share simply illustrate my amazement that I survived. But more importantly, they show the truth that, through every single moment of my life, even when I did not realize it, God had a plan for me. He helped me get through and learn time and again. He's still doing that in my life today. I truly believe, deep within my being, that God has a plan for me. I was not in any way a mistake, and He has been preparing me to do what He created me to do.

One main factor that rang true throughout my life was

that I always saw myself as part of the answer. Let's take a moment and dig into this belief. Let's think about the world and all the problems that exist within it. My simple question to you is: Are you part of the problem or are you part of the answer? I truly believe a lot of your decision-making could fall into one of those two categories. So, if you'll answer that question ("Am I part of the problem or the answer?") when you choose to do something, I believe it will help you make the right decision. Another simple question I've learned to ask myself (that I probably should have asked many more times than I did) is, what good can come from this? Seriously, if I do this, what good can come from it? This is a question I wish I had asked more in my life.

So, in this book, I'm going to share with you a few stories from my childhood, my teens, and my early twenties. Through these experiences, I'll share lessons I've learned and some of the lessons I should have learned. Hopefully you can identify with these experiences and maybe learn some fresh lessons as well.

Let me take a moment and set the stage, providing a little background before I just dive into my stories. I need to clearly explain the setting, the obstacles, and the realities that existed. However, please remember that my main purpose in writing this book is to try and encourage, motivate or inspire fellow dads to man up and start striving to be part of the answer! I believe we all have a story to tell and when you understand another person's story, it can help you better understand who they are and who they are trying to become. A person's story is like a road map. Many times, when we put in that GPS address, it gives us the fastest way or a route without toll roads or one that stays on major highways. I believe this illustration can help us approach our decision-making. We often know where we want to go in life, but the problem is there are so many routes from which to choose. So, we begin our journey and have no idea how some uneducated and easy decisions can take us completely off the beaten path and down a road that is entirely under construction. It's a road we should have never ventured down to begin with. Now, as we come to one of our first crossroads or navigational decisions, we must consider the following:

- Do we keep going in hopes that it is going to get better?
- Should we turn around now in hopes that we just cut our losses and get back on a better path?
- Do we keep going with the belief that there is no possible way it could get worse?

We make these decisions all the time in relationships and friendships. Sometimes they work out and sometimes they do not. We may envision our decisions all working out beautifully, as if we are living in a Hollywood TV series, that wraps everything up in a bow by the end of the episode. But that's not always the case in real life. For example, we may decide to support a friend or loved one, and that relationship takes us down a dangerous road, further than we thought or intended to go.

As people, as men, as dads, we need to own our decisions and the directions we choose to go. Picture being on a road trip with someone in your passenger seat (we'll call this person your co-pilot) and a GPS you have programmed. You are ready to go. As you get further down the road, the GPS shows you a wreck along your route. You're coming upon it quickly. You may ask your co-pilot if they believe you should take the alternate route the GPS suggests or stick with the main route, believing the congestion will clear up soon. It's an immediate question requiring an immediate answer as the exit is coming up in two miles!

With the pressure of the question, your co-pilot may have a few different reactions.

- "OMG… does he want me to make the decision for him? I don't want that responsibility and especially the blame, if it's the wrong choice." So, the co-pilot decides to say nothing.
- "Wait, I have not been paying attention and cannot make that decision in the next two minutes!" So, the co-pilot pleads the fifth.
- "I think you should stay/take the exit." The co-pilot has been paying attention and has an educated opinion.

This situation could lead to nothing; your decision worked out and you never thought of the conversation again. However, if you followed the suggestion of your co-pilot and got negative results, then it's likely you will never forget this decision.

The point of this imaginative exercise is ownership. Ultimately, as dads, we need to take ownership of our decisions regardless of the positive or negative outcomes. Although, in this situation we may have asked for our co-pilot's opinion, we ultimately made the decision, and the positive or negative outcome belongs to us. This is called accountability, and at the end of the day we need to be more accountable to our families.

I would love to think I do this regularly today, but it took me a long time to learn this lesson.

In our own stories, we are defined by experiences, actions, consequences, and things that happen to us as we are developing, learning, and growing. Some of the end results are things we brought on ourselves, but sometimes we simply find ourselves part of the collateral damage of circumstances outside our control.

To truly understand someone's story, we need to know how it all started. Context always helps. It's hard to go much farther back for context than birth. We all have a father, or a sperm donor as some may consider. My father, Jerry, was married to my mother for about four or five years. Then my mother introduced us to our first stepfather, Alan, who invaded our home straight from Vietnam. He drank scotch on the rocks every day and beat the fool out of my mom for about three years. Male influence No. 3, Larry, seemed to be a better guy who was into hunting and fishing. I was excited as I'd never had the chance to do those kinds of things and, as a child, I really enjoyed it. However, Larry had his own demons, and you will hear about that soon enough. The fourth inside-the-home male influence, Jim, was introduced later in my life, when I was 19 or 20, and by that time, I was out of the home for the most part.

So, you can see how I arrived at that place of internal questioning when we were expecting our first child. With the track record of fathers in my life, of course I felt ill-equipped and wondered how to figure this fatherhood thing out. No one can solve this puzzle of fatherhood on their own. When you don't know what constitutes a good functional family, but you do know what it takes to conjure up a dysfunctional one, how can you navigate the mine field of decision-making without destroying the home you are trying to build?

In my opinion, you must start with the man in the mirror. Do the internal work to determine those morals, values and ethics that are worth passing on to your children. Some of these lessons you'll learn simply by observation and some of these lessons you'll learn through positive male role models in your own life (if you're fortunate enough to have those). However, some of these things you'll simply learn by trial and error. Unfortunately, it's in those clueless decision-making times that you usually hurt those around you the most. It's those loved ones or friends who truly care about you, who probably suffer the most. As you rationalize the reasoning behind your unwise decisions, some of the stupid things you do in the name of pride, self-respect, or insecurity are astonishing.

The excuses are as endless as the stars in the sky. There are times you believe you're getting disrespected, and your answer is to be rude to the people closest to you. Then, there are other times you are simply ignorant. I owe the biggest apologies to those friends and loved ones I've done wrong over the years. As I reflect upon those thousands of impulsive and bad decisions I have made, I would give anything to be able to go back and correct them. The number of impulsive things I did is endless, and the wreckage I left in my formative years is massive. It's those friends and family members to whom I owe the biggest apologies. Unfortunately, those things cannot be undone. Thankfully, I had developed enough street credit with those people that they saw through my impulsiveness or stupidity and loved me through those situations. To those people who stood by me when they probably should not have, I am forever indebted and want to say thank you for caring and loving me when I was, frankly, not acting as someone worthy of time or energy.

Hopefully, through these next chapters, I might jog a memory in your own mind or maybe just make you think.

But, at the end of all this, I just hope you choose to be part of the answer and not part of the problem. I'm grateful you are still reading. I'll close with a challenge: go back to those people who helped you survive and tell them "Thank you" for caring about you when you didn't deserve it. Trust me, you did not get where you are on your own. I am sure there was a tenth-grade teacher who spoke life into you or a youth soccer coach who saw something in you that you did not see in yourself. Whoever these people are for you, they inspired you to become something you did not believe possible. I promise you that it will be worth your time to go thank them, even if you shed a tear. I hope through these stories, you think about your own life and develop even more courage to be a good dad, mentor or husband.

Are you ready? Let's Goooooo!

Understanding the Chapters

In the proceeding chapters I am going to share stories that shaped and molded my childhood and early adult years. These experiences helped shape the father I became.

The premise of the book is that we all play for a team in life. When you are born, you play for whatever team your parents are on. As life progresses, you get to decide which team you will eventually play for. (When I was born, I joined the *Trailer Park White Trash* team; but as I got older, I left that team and joined the *Dad Legends* team. I will explain more about this later.)

When you're on a team in school, you get a letter jacket. Since we are on a team in life, then we should have a letter jacket. If we have a letter jacket, then we must have patches we earn for our letter jacket. After each story, there is a section called "The Patch," in which I explain the patch I earned from the negative, painful lessons that I wore on my *Trailer Park White Trash* jacket. Following the negative, I will give insight into how this painful experience became a positive force for change in my own life and resulted in a much different patch on my *Dad Legends* jacket. Following these, I share a one-line principle that I apply to my life to help guide me through the snares and pitfalls of decision-making. I hope these principles can provide guidance and motivation during your dad journey, as well.

At the end of each story, in a section called "Huddle-up," I reflect on what lesson I learned or how I should have managed situations differently. Remember, a huddle is when we all come together in a quick circle on the football field to share some information (for instance, to call a play or to motivate one another). I simply share my thoughts and the effects or fallout of each event.

The first few chapters are about experiences in my early childhood (when I was on the *Trailer Park White Trash* team*)* and the latter chapters are about experiences from my late teens to early twenties, as I mentally began to prepare myself to join the right team—*The Dad Legends*.

I hope you enjoy this book and, more importantly, I hope you desire to join the *Dad Legends* and make a strong difference in your children's lives.

Let's Go! One chapter at a time!

CHAPTER 1

THE TREASURE HUNT CHRISTMAS

As I begin this story, I want to explain that things around our household were, let's just say, *different* at times. To borrow a line from *Dumb and Dumber*, "Just when I think you could not go any lower, you totally redeem yourself." My mother always had the innate ability to take any situation and hit a single (notice I did not say "home run") or totally strike out.

In the winter of 1978, after the leaves fell and the cold crept upon us, Christmas was quickly approaching. We lived in a trailer at this time, as we had for most of my life. During the gift-giving season, my sister and I had always kept a rather reserved approach to asking for gifts from our mother. We were fully aware that funds were limited. Even as children, we were aware of our financial state; after all, we knew where we lived!

Before I tell this entire story, you need a little background information to genuinely appreciate everything that transpired. My mother was, shall we say, a special woman. Like many women who get married and have children at an early age (18 for her), she had missed her young adult years of going out/dating. She was quickly making up for that loss during my early childhood years. She had several sayings that she liked to share with anyone willing to lend an ear. Certain sayings pretty much summed up our situation. They ranged from, "Po, but Proud," to "If the wolf had come to our house, he would have had to bring a sack lunch" to the most notorious, intoxicated saying, "That's my boy! Raised him on milk of magnesia. Ain't he the sh**s." These sayings can shine some clarifying light on our lives at that time; but the depth of the insanity will soon reveal itself as you read.

As I was saying, Christmas was approaching. I had not asked for anything except a bicycle. I did not expect a fancy BMX ride; just a cheap-o bike from K-mart (when it used to exist). My mom had not said much about the bike. With her uncanny ability to pull something special out of her hat during Christmas time, I had no reason to expect anything other than a bike.

Our custom was to open presents at home on Christmas Eve. That fateful night, we all sat around the tree to exchange the small presents we had for each other. It was also a custom to have the youngest child open presents first and then the next youngest, and so on. I was first—one of the only advantages to being the younger sibling that I can remember (but it was huge this time of year). My mother brought me the biggest gift I had ever seen. The box was huge—nearly four feet square! I wondered how she managed to cram my bicycle into that cardboard container. She was a genius, a magician! She was the best. I ripped the paper to shreds. The box had a big Charmin logo on the side. I didn't remember Charmin making bicycles, but I knew there was a bicycle in that box. When I opened the cardboard container, I was greeted by a lot of newspapers inside. Hidden in the newspaper was a small, wrapped present. It held a small scroll that read:

Hickory, Dickory, Dock
It's time to race against the Clock.
Be sure not to be late,
As the next clue may disintegrate.
Move 10 paces in a scamper,
So, hurry and check the bathroom hamper.

Oh, my goodness, it was on! Throwing the Charmin box out of my way, I raced toward the next clue. Down the hall and into the bathroom I did, in fact, scamper. I threw the dirty clothes from the hamper all over the room and, lo and behold, there was another box. Ripping the paper to shreds, I opened it and read the next clue.

Jack and Jill went up the hill to fetch a pail of water,
Jack fell down and broke his crown and Jill came tumbling after.
Time is running out,
Your next clue is near the spout.
Turn around and go back to dinner,
As you will find your clue when you enter.

Leaving the mess behind me, I raced toward the kitchen at the other end of our mobile home. The note had said, "You will find the clue when you enter." However, the treasure I yearned for did not appear near the doorway. I looked back at my mom, who beamed with excitement, and asked her, "Where is it?" She told me to read the clue again. I glanced back over it and realized that the present had to be somewhere near the kitchen sink. The prize I sought was not in plain view there, either. It had to be here somewhere nearby, but where? Then it dawned on me, it had to be under the sink! Sure enough, there it was right next to the Comet cleaner. I grabbed the box and tore it open like a cannibal looking for a meal. Inside was another one of those riddles. Part of me was excited, the other part exasperated; nonetheless, I opened the scroll and began reading.

T'was the night before Christmas and all through the house
Not a creature was stirring, not even a mouse.
It won't be much longer, so do not delay,
The next clue to be sought is on the way.
I do not have many more words to mutter,
Move back down the hall to a room with clutter.
Be sure to look around to find the clue,
It's in the corner where you find your shoe.

As much fun as I had with this scavenger hunt, the anticipation drove me crazy. My mind continued to race about what my mother could have gotten me that would be worthy of this type of work and effort. She had really outdone herself with the clues and these small presents. I knew we did not have much, as far as worldly possessions were concerned, but her efforts to make this Christmas special were a treasure in and of themselves.

I raced back down the hall to the second door on the left and entered the "room with clutter" (my room). Obviously, the shoes clue led me to the closet, and I began to throw shoes, clothes, and anything else out of my way to find this mystery present. Much to my liking, I spotted another scroll in the corner. This one was not in a box but simply wrapped with a string holding it closed. I quickly untied it and began to read.

There is not time to waste,
It's time to make haste.
Go to the container next to the door,
You know the one, it has many a drawer.
The big surprise will happen in a minute,
It is the drawer with T-shirts in it.

My mother was a genius. She had told us funds were limited, but she was turning this into the best present ever. The clue led me to my dresser, and I knew exactly which drawer she described, the fourth one. I stepped over and opened it. I did not see anything. As I turned to look at my mother, her eyes were beginning to fill with tears. I knew whatever she had gotten me this year was really special, as she had devoted an extraordinary amount of time and thought into this gift. She motioned for me to keep looking in the drawer, and I obliged her. Sure enough, under the shirts, there was another wrapped present in a box about ten by twelve inches and about an inch thick. Anticipating yet another scroll inside, I opened the box. The next moment was burned into my memory, much like the misery old people talk about when they describe The Great Depression, or the ability people have to describe exactly what they were doing when they learned about 9/11. I pulled the lid off the box and what was inside was revealed.

I twisted my head to look at my mother so quickly that I must have appeared to be possessed. When our eyes met, I could tell that she had been holding back her tears of joy, anticipation, and happiness. She threw her arms around me and the tears flowed. I also began to sob, but for an entirely different reason. The more she cried the more I cried. After a few moments, we gathered ourselves, and I investigated the box again. I did all I could to not burst into tears again when she reached into the box and removed the framed portrait of herself and placed it onto my chest of drawers. Without missing a beat, she turned and said, "You know I am not going to live forever, and there will be a day when you will want a picture of me to look at when I am dead and gone."

I burst into tears again. While true that it is important to hold to memories and pictures of your parents, or stories told about them when they pass, my mother was only in her thirties at this time. Even now, this seems such a strange gift for a young boy.

For the rest of that night, I could not stop thinking about what I was going to tell my friends at school about my Christmas gifts. I had to come up with something. I could see it play out in my mind. All the guys would be standing in a circle at recess; David would start talking about the bike he received. Chris would talk about his train. Then they would turn to me and ask what I had received. Usually, at this time in the thought or dream, I would wake up or forcefully turn my mind from the embarrassment I expected. What would I say? An 8 x 10 of my mother? Really? I would be the laughingstock of the fourth grade. I had to produce something. I finally settled on saying I had received a bike. Then, I would follow that up with the news it had been stolen.

THE PATCH

The letter jacket patch that adorned my *Trailer Park White Trash* jacket as a result of this experience was an **E for embarrassment.**

I am not sure anyone in the world wants to experience embarrassment. Webster's dictionary defines embarrassment as, "a feeling of self-consciousness, shame, or awkwardness." There were times in my childhood that embarrassment is not a strong enough word to describe the feelings I had when I was around my mother. No child should have to experience being embarrassed by the behavior of their parent.

My sister and I spent countless hours at athletic events, the lake, or some random Friday or Saturday at home surviving an alcohol-induced moment; our parent being loud and drawing attention was a rite of passage. We would make eye contact, sometimes acknowledging what was about to happen, while other times, we simply expressed shock and amazement. You know, there is nothing like having your parent do something outlandish while you make eye contact with someone in the room who is looking at you as if to say, "Are you not embarrassed? Aren't you going to stop this?" Meanwhile, you're thinking, "Does the child have to be the adult, yet one more time?"

I know that every one of you have experienced embarrassment and the feeling that you just wanted to run away and hide. The degree of embarrassment does not matter, but what does matter is the feeling that came over you when you experienced it. Take a moment and see if you relate to any of the following incidents:

Giving a wrong answer aloud in class.

While reading aloud, mispronouncing a word.

Making a stupid error during a sporting event.

Dropping something in the cafeteria, making a mess, and having all eyes on you.

Entering the wrong room for a meeting.

Having your name announced over the loudspeaker . . . and not for a good reason.

All of these situations describe an embarrassing moment, and we can all relate to that paralyzing feeling. However, it enters an entirely different realm when embarrassment goes from an event to a lifestyle. This is what happened to me and my sister in our youth. I realized early on that the circumstance of my childhood did not need to be my future destiny. I did not like the feeling of being embarrassed, attention being drawn to us and all that comes with sticking out in a crowd. I admit I became somewhat numb to it, but still it was not a life experience I wanted to pass on to my children.

This Patch was powerful. I found I could not escape the embarrassment my mother embraced. That "poor but proud" saying she engrained in our brains was not humorous to me, and I saw little of which to be proud. The stunts she pulled and questionable things she did are too numerous to count. No child should have to live through continual embarrassment produced by their parents' behavior or actions. The exposure to this embarrassment provided two things for me:

1. I became callus to certain behaviors and could hardly be shocked (as I felt like I had seen it all)
2. I became cold and resentful toward my mom.

As you analyze your own life, think about situations or experiences that made you feel uncomfortable. Not everyone's life is colored by ongoing, major embarrassment. In your own life, maybe it was abuse or toxicity that overtook your young years. Realize those years are gone, and you need no longer be a victim of poor choices by parents or care givers. Learn the lesson the difficulties taught and employ them to make you better, not bitter.

My past set me up for bitterness and failure. But I chose to rise above the things I could not change. I have now exchanged the "E" patch for a very different one. My *Dad Legends* jacket proudly displays an **E for expectation**. A lifestyle of embarrassment caused me to hide from life. It caused a great deal of bitterness and a fatalistic way of viewing the world around me. A worldview of expectation replaces the "what next" of dread with the "what next" of anticipation.

The Principle I want to teach and hope to pass on to you is:

Your current circumstances do not determine your future destination.

Please listen to me about this. With hard work and time, you can overcome any circumstance that has negatively impacted your life.

Huddle Up

You know, I should have done a better job of realizing my mother was doing the best she could at the time, especially because times were hard!

I have often thought back over this event and really been at a loss for words. Seriously. Did my mother really think I would want a picture of her for Christmas, when I was in the fourth grade? Honestly, what was her rationale for this decision?

I do believe my mother had a great heart and always meant well, but sometimes the result was puzzling. Confusing? Astonishing? Amazing? All these words apply. Again, I believe she did the best with what she had, although she sometimes rationalized, manipulating the means to justify the end result. As an adult, I was very troubled when I started to analyze my childhood and some of the situations she put my sister and me in. Without a doubt, the more I compared how I wanted to raise my children and how she chose to raise us, the more deeply it affected my relationship with her. I loved her for everything she did for us, but I elected to distance my family from the chaos she chose to have around her at any and all given moments.

It's a good thing to love your parents for who they are, but sometimes you must make hard decisions for your own family to protect them from the unpredictable world around them. Unfortunately, those decisions may affect your relationship with your parents. However, at the end of the day, God gave you children and gave you the responsibility to raise them the way you deem fit, as you follow Him. When all is said and done, I am responsible for my children, and it's my charge to keep them in a safe and healthy environment. I believe it is our job to get our kids to 18 with as few negative, life-changing events as possible.

CHAPTER 2

YOU GOTTA KNOW WHEN TO HOLD 'EM...

If memory serves, Allen Coker was introduced to my family back in the mid '70s and he was nothing like any man my sister and I had ever met. At about six feet tall and 230 pounds, he was a big man. The main thing I remember about him is that he always had a glass of scotch on the rocks in his hand. He was physically in Knoxville, Tennessee, but mentally he was still in Vietnam, fighting "Charlie." Except now, Charlie lived in a trailer and had two small children, Suzanne and Greg, living with her.

It's hard to define the role Allen had in our family. There was a time when my mother introduced him to us as our stepfather. Then, later on (after my mom had left him), she explained she had not actually been married to him those first few years. So, to say the least, it was complex and confusing to us.

They were together for around three years. Due to mental and physical brutality, it seemed more like decades. I remember that he woke up drinking and went to bed drinking; the worst part was that some of those drunken days were violent. I am talking about the kind of violence no child is prepared to see nor live through. My mother thought she was doing what was best or right in her eyes, but we begged her to leave him; she always had a reason we or she could not. However, being a 9- or 10-year-old kid and seeing your mother have her jaw broken from a hit by your supposed stepfather was frightening and beyond the coping ability of a child. I have no way of knowing how many times this kind of thing happened. However, I have memories of running for our lives from drunken rages and other extremely frightening situations. I remember one night during those years when my mother asked me why I was sleeping in my clothes. I told her I wanted to save time in the morning; but the reality was, the nightly arguing often became violent, and I was not sure what was going to happen as I slept. So, I chose to sleep in my clothes in case I had to run out the back door before morning. I will try to recount a few of these situations so you may get a better picture of the insanity that surrounded us.

We had lived in the trailer park for a few years. There is a hierarchy in the trailer park world. At that time, if you had a double-wide trailer, you were like the Clampetts (from the Beverly Hillbillies); just the high-class white trash. Those TP owners who had the financial means to hide their wheels (folks who could afford underpinning) were a little higher in the trailer park caste. Then there were the rest of us. We lived in a trailer with exposed wheels, meaning we were ready to move at a moment's notice. We were at the bottom of the TP hierarchy.

Another sad reality in the TP environment is families live in survival mode–a different set of morals and values in which the end is justified by whatever means necessary. To explain further, lying might have been necessary to get the desirable end; but if it worked out positively for the family, it was acceptable. Cheating a bit to get a good result wasn't a problem. All people in this type of situation have their own set of standards and rules that are specific to their family. Some may say, "We might be poor, but we are not thieves or liars." However, where they stand on one value or another can be as changeable as the wind, and their willingness to break their own code of conduct can be easily justified if doing so creates a positive result.

This was the reality in our family during the Allen years. Too many times, Allen was drunk, which led to arguments and late-night free-for-alls. As a result, my sister and I would spend a lot of time at our grandmother's home. She lived in the country, and her home was always safe. I remember when I was nine and entering my first year of Little League (at this time the age range in Little League went from 9–12). I had just graduated from T-ball in which you hit a stationary ball off a stand and run like the wind around the bases. This Little League thing was a whole new adventure, and I didn't have anyone at home to help me make the transition. "Stepfather" Allen told my mom he would be more than glad to help me learn how to hit a pitched ball, since my biggest issue was being afraid those big 12-year-old pitchers were going to hit me with the ball. This fear would cause me to get "happy feet" and do everything but leave the batter's box whenever the pitcher started winding up. (Honestly, this is somewhat normal for a kid who has never experienced anything like kid-pitch before, but this was not acceptable in 1977.) Allen said, "Let's go hit!" and we all loaded into the car. We drove over to the Little League park and luckily (or unluckily, for me), there was no one else there. Allen grabbed some balls and said, "Let's go, boy." I was completely clueless, but I knew enough to know that this was not going to be a positive experience.

This huge, scotch-smelling, Vietnam vet was facing me from the mound, toeing the rubber, ready to show me his fast ball. (Let me remind you, I was 9 years old.) I was starting to whimper like a little pup that just peed in the kitchen and knows he is about to get hit with the newspaper again. My desire to live and not get hit with this guy's fast ball was overtaking my desire to be a successful Little League hitter. I am sure Allen had every intention of throwing strikes and proving to the VFW that he could teach me to hit, but when the first two pitches he threw hit halfway up the backstop, my happy feet hit another level. At this moment, I felt like Michael Jackson in that batter's box. My whole body was shaking. He was yelling at me and calling me scared. I was calculating the odds of him throwing a strike vs. him hitting me in the side of the head with the next pitch or two ... it really was just a matter of time. (Looking back, I am not sure why I was scared. I mean, I *was* wearing one of those Cincinnati Reds helmets you buy at K-mart, and it would certainly have protected me from his 75-mph fastball.) I am sure this hitting lesson probably took no longer than half an hour, but after standing in the batter's box and feeling like I was playing fast-pitch dodgeball, it felt more like several hours. Needless to say, I did not learn much about hitting that day; but I felt a lot better about my ability to get out of the way of a ball thrown at my head or back by some big 12-year-old.

One evening, Allen wanted to play poker and his buddy, Jake, sat down to play with us. As a bit of background, at about the age of 6 or 7, my real father taught me how to play cards. I am not talking about five- or seven-card stud or anything like that, but he had taught me gin rummy and other simple card games. My father liked to gamble and deal cards at a local gambling spot. He made sure I had a basic background with the fundamentals of cards.

Allen decided he wanted us to play with poker chips; all of us put $5 in and then got $5 worth of chips. Red chips equaled 25 cents, white equaled 10 cents and blue equaled 5 cents We were playing seven-card stud, with nothing wild. For those of you unfamiliar, this is basically Texas Hold 'Em of today, without a dealer. You get two cards down, then you bet. Next, you receive four cards up, betting after each card you receive. Finally, you get one card down at the end (or on the river).

We had been playing for a while, and I was barely surviving. My money was low, and Allen was bragging about his superior card play to me and Jake. At one point, I was out of money, and he volunteered to float me $5 more worth of chips. Of course, I already owed him. We kept playing, and I felt like I was in the fight of my life. If I kept losing, I was going to have to wash the dishes every night the next week, among other penalties. While one particular hand was progressing as normal, we reached our five cards, and I had two kings showing and Allen had two aces showing. This erstwhile Little League hitting instructor believed he could run me out of money, so he kept raising and making me use my money to stay in the game. What he did not know was that I had a king in the hole (one of my two "down" cards) and I was sitting on three of a kind while he only had a pair of aces showing. You may be wondering how I knew this.

Earlier in this chapter, I talked about self-preservation. It is more of an instinct than you can believe. Living, breathing, and not getting the SH#$ beat out of you were unbelievable motivators for success. My sister and I learned survival skills that were not necessarily taught along with spelling or math in school. Natural survival instincts kicked in naturally and instinctively. Our mother didn't teach us these things, but we observed her behavior. We saw how she sometimes would rationalize things that did not seem right to us but worked out in our favor. It was those kinds of things we learned.

I put those survival skills to work as I sweated my way through this card-game fiasco and the poker sun shined on me, so to speak. I discovered a little advantage: Allen would sometimes be a little sloppy with his cards. If he sat in a certain chair and held his cards just right, their reflection in the toaster behind him would reveal to me what he had in his hand. If this didn't work, I had a back-up plan. He wore thick glasses and if the light was just right, you could look into his glasses when he peaked at his cards and see what he had in the hole. We were coming down to the last card, the seventh one, and it would be down. I had already bet all my remaining money and told Allen I was all in. I knew I had three kings; Allen had a pair of aces showing. We received our last card; but instead of looking at my card when I got it, I looked into Allen's glasses to see what his last card was. He drew a four of clubs and was stuck with a pair of aces. I asked Allen what he was going to do. He looked at me and said, "Kid, I hit trip aces, but I don't want to take your money, and I am going to fold." No quicker did he get that out of his mouth than I reached over and said "No, you don't," and I flipped his cards over, exposing the fact that he was lying. Before I could move another inch, he backhanded me out of my chair and told me, "If this was a real poker game, I would have shot you for doing that." I landed in the middle of the living room, got up crying, then raked all the chips back to my side of the table and began counting my winnings. It remained quiet as I paid him back his $5, claimed my own $5, plus an additional $3.

In all the time I knew him, Allen was a wreck. He created some memories that I am sure I have deleted or hidden in a file so deep inside my memory that it would take a month of visits to the psychologist to pull them out of me. Another one I remember happened the summer after fifth grade. Mom had decided we were moving to Orlando to get a fresh start with Allen. Suzanne and I knew that if scotch could be sold in Orlando, then the same problems were sure to follow us. I remember we moved to an apartment complex, went swimming most days, and it usually rained every afternoon. Allen was apparently trying to make an honest living being a pest-control guy and driving some sort of car outfitted with a mouse on top.

It had been a couple of months since he had gone bonkers, so the law of averages was not working in our favor. We were all walking around on eggshells, hoping every day that this would not be *the* day. One random morning, the day we dreaded arrived. We (Suzanne, my mom, and me) had been hanging at the pool and having a good ole time when Mr. Mouse came home in a tizzy. Suzanne and I had no idea what was wrong, but we knew to be on alert; there was no telling who would be the target of his wrath. Mom had made spaghetti, our favorite, and we all sat down to share the meal. I was a sloppy eater at best; when one of the spaghetti noodles was left dangling from my mouth, I thought nothing about slurping it up. Well, that day was not the day to be careless with my eating. After one of my slurping incidents, Allen told me that I had better not do that again. It registered in my head for a moment but not long enough to make a lasting impact. My lapse would be quickly corrected. A few more minutes went by and, low and behold, I had forgotten the instructions Allen had just decreed. I slurped up another noodle or two to keep them from hanging on my chin.

No sooner had that the spaghetti landed on my tongue than Allen grabbed the food out of my plate and hit me in the face with it. Shock and awe are the only words to describe what happened next—Allen got up, said he was tired of this *stuff*, and jerked the tablecloth and our entire meal off the table and onto the floor. We were all in shock at this moment and more than a little afraid his anger would escalate, and he might become more violent. He was well on his way into rage when, for the first time, my mom picked up the phone and called the police. They showed up and took him outside. My mother called her mom and uncle, and they agreed to front her the money to get us home. Suddenly, we had thirty minutes to pack everything we wanted to take, but it all had to fit into an airport travel box. We hurried around and got our stuff together, and the police escorted us to the taxi. We moved back home that very night.

Allen had terrorized Suzanne and me, but thankfully this chapter of our lives seemed to be ending. Unfortunately, once we returned to Halls Crossroads, it appeared that some lessons are never learned as we moved into another trailer in another part of the trailer park. I can only figure this is all that my mother could afford on her secretary's income, since my father never once paid child support to help her. Then, too, I now realize that some people fall back into their own financial or moral patterns when given a choice between the tough road or the easy one. I believe she was doing what she thought was best for us but nonetheless, it was déjà vu all over again.

Allen resumed his reign of terror. He ran us off the road, shot at us with a shotgun, and did many other traumatizing things not worth recalling. He also hit my mother many times. Many of these attacks happened because my mother started dating another man, named Larry. However, Larry had been a police officer and somehow, some way, all of Allen's shenanigans came to a quick end once Larry showed up in the picture.

If I am not mistaken, we moved eleven or twelve times during my childhood, but mostly within that small Halls Crossroads community, north of Knoxville. While there is comfort to be found in the familiar, life was chaotic for most of my childhood. Once we moved back to the trailer park, some other things began to happen with me. I was starting to grow up—puberty was entering the picture. I began developing a temper and feelings of protectiveness for my mother grew stronger. These became major factors in our family experiences moving forward.

THE PATCH

The letter jacket patch I earned through this experience and pinned to my *Trailer Park White Trash* jacket was a dollar sign **($)**, signifying **moral and ethical bankruptcy**.

Kids who grow up in settings such as I did, begin to anticipate the next bad situation and are on the lookout for any brewing crisis. They have a hard time relaxing because they are so used to having to manage their own lives through chaos. The fight-or-flight defensive mechanism becomes honed while surviving the day or moment becomes the most important pursuit. Making it through the day, the hour, or the minute—once the wheels start coming off—is uppermost in their minds and hearts. They learn to say or do whatever is necessary to survive, and the need for self-justification begins to prompt an ever-deepening moral decay. They will do what they need to do to survive—survival is the win. They're not necessarily taught this. Maybe they observe their parents or people around them make compromising moral decisions and model that behavior. Or perhaps it becomes a gradual slippery slope. Regardless of what happens first, the cycle begins and repeats.

As I got older, I began to realize that my morals and values did not have a compass. I justified my actions as a child based solely on self-preservation. I believe many children who grow up in lower, socio-economic situations share a common bond here. Minute-by-minute survival holds greater importance than the consequences tomorrow may bring. However, not having a moral compass leads to a life without direction. The moral decay, unless corrected, will destroy relationships through the lies, cheating, and stealing used to generate a positive result in the end. The ends justify the means.

The $ on my *Trailer Park White Trash* jacket was transferred to my *Dad Legends* jacket. However, the meaning changed radically. It no longer stands for moral and ethical bankruptcy; it now represents the value of my life and every life. Once you acknowledge that every life is priceless and every person is created for a specific purpose only they can fulfill, it is no longer reasonable to enter into degrading, devaluing actions and attitudes. What happened yesterday need not define today. You can recognize destructive, old patterns and get them under control. No one is bound to yesterday. Radical changes in behavior and a conscientious decision to change priorities will drastically change the future! Develop your moral compass and allow it to guide your life, for without it, you are like a rudderless boat in a hurricane. Your purpose is to lead, and no one will ever follow you if you are blown about by every contrary wind.

Without a moral compass to guide your life, you become a rudderless boat in a hurricane, and no one will ever follow you.

I discovered that telling the truth simplifies life. Being determined to live with principles and strong beliefs creates a life that is solid, secure, and orderly. When I decided hard work would be a value that defined me, it was not hard to challenge my children to do the same. This is true of all the virtues I determined to adopt in my adult life. Consistent morals and values allow you to make consistent decisions regardless of who is involved.

The principle I want to pass on to you is this:

To be a dad of whom your children are proud, you have to become a man worth following.

Huddle Up

I believe most every child is born with an innate instinct to survive and want to stay out of trouble. For example, you can throw a baby into a pool, and they will naturally try to swim or float to survive; they do not just sink to the bottom without a fight. Survival is an instinct; it does not have to be taught. Without much coercing, children will lie, cheat, or steal to survive their day. They may not do this on day one, but as they grow, whenever they experience an unfulfilled need, they will naturally do whatever it takes to survive. I share this because it's our job as the dads in our homes to create an environment in which our children do not need to learn these dubious skills. It is our job to correct them when they lie. When we catch them cheating, we need to work hard to teach them why it is important to be honest. If they steal, we must teach them the meaning of honoring others.

If we do not carry the banner for strong morals, values, and ethics, then we are just continuing to allow the problems of the world to continue. Be strong and be consistent. Those are just two keys to creating a healthy environment for your children. Remember, all of this starts with you. You may well need to work on strengthening those qualities within yourself. It's all part of the job.

Chapter 3

My First (and only) BB gun

My mom and a man named Larry had been married for a few years, and he had proven to be the most loving example of a father I had experienced up until that point. His wife had died during childbirth, and my mom gladly stepped into the void her passing had left. Larry's commitment to my mom brought with it a ready-made family: my 13-year-old sister, Suzanne, and 12-year-old me. Larry embraced all of us with open arms; Suzanne and I could not have dreamed of a better life situation. What a welcome change Larry's brand of love was from what we had known at the hands of Allen.

During the first few years, Larry took me fishing and hunting with him. He took his time and taught me with patience and care. I genuinely believed that he cared about my well-being and wanted to teach me the right ways to hunt and fish. Larry did not give a half-hearted effort—his actions made me believe he wanted to be a loving, caring dad . . . *my* loving, caring dad.

I remember when he thought it was time for me to learn how to mow the grass. I was all for it until he told me I was going to be cutting the back yard with his riding lawn mower. I was petrified. It was a big, expensive machine. I worried about what would happen if I damaged it in some way I feared he would go crazy and give me one of those "Allen" types of whippings. Even though he was more than confident I could handle the task, I was not. He educated me on what made it go, stop, how to engage the mower, lower the blade and all I needed to know to operate the fearful machine. My 5-minute tutorial went through one ear and out the other; but off I went, cutting the grass. I made big squares, following the fence that enclosed the back yard. Shockingly, I found the machine responsive, and I seemed to be doing a fine job. All I had to do was line up my wheels in the same track as the round before, and I would not miss any spots. It was child's play, and I felt my confidence soar. I had made about five treks around the yard when I realized my next turn would put me on course to hit the back of Larry's boat, parked off to the side of the yard. Larry was busy in another area of the yard, and I began wishing I had paid closer attention to his instructions. I started stomping on the brake with all my 12-year-old strength, but the mower kept moving forward— ever closer to Larry's prized possession. Panic seized me; I was not going to be able to avoid disaster. Larry looked in my direction just in time to see me hit the back tail light; the mower just kept spinning in place, trying to continue its path. I jumped off the mower and turned it off. I was filled with dread about what would happen next. I expected this guy to come flying towards me with anger-crazed eyes and fists swinging, but he did not. He simply walked over, looked at the damage, and asked, "Did you forget to push in the clutch? It won't stop, if you don't." I said, "Yes sir. I guess I did. I'm sorry for the damage to your boat." Then I slumped over, waiting for the backhand I knew was coming . . . or maybe even a worse consequence. Larry asked, "What are you doing?" Straightening up, I said, "I thought you would be mad." He looked at me with true concern and said, "Are you serious? That piece of plastic can be replaced. I am just glad I was here, and you are okay." I knew in that moment that this guy was different.

During the summer before my seventh-grade year, Larry brought home a BB gun. I wasn't familiar with any gun, BB or otherwise. This particular gun was a one-pump model, meaning that only one pump was needed to prepare it to shoot. (There is type that must be pumped multiple times. The more pumps, the further and harder it propels the BB.) Larry taught me how to load the BB gun. I loaded it with about fifty BBs and felt excitement building.

I was ready to shoot but wasn't sure what or where. I asked Larry and he told me I needed to practice shooting at a target. I went inside and drew a bullseye on a paper plate. I took it outside and fastened it to the chain link fence. I then walked back fifteen paces, turned around, pumped the gun, and fired. Much to my amazement, I was awful. I shot a few times, walked up to the fence and, sure enough, I had missed the paper plate target every time. I walked back, made some adjustments, then pumped and fired multiple shots again. I missed the mark every single time. I thought to myself, "The birds in this neighborhood are safe!"

I continued practicing and, surprisingly, I improved over the next thirty or so shots. I was beginning to hear the slightly muffled sound of the BB's hitting the paper plate. However, as I took a few more shots, I realized I no longer heard the sound of BB's hitting the target. I was befuddled. I began to shoot and take a step forward, shoot and take a step forward until I was just a few steps away from the target. The sound of BB's hitting the thin cardboard had been absent following every shot. Feeling confused, I took another few shots and then realized the chamber must be empty of BBs. I continued to pump and shoot just to make sure. Feeling the need to verify the gun was empty, I walked up to the target and placed the gun about ten inches away, pumped, and pulled the trigger. The shot caused a large, black smudge on the white target. "Really cool!" I thought. I pumped and pulled the trigger again; *BOOM!* another black mark. Too Cool!

Then, the most inexplicable thought entered my mind: "I wonder if it would make a black mark on my hand?" Looking back, I realize this thought was neither sane nor safe, but back then, my curiosity outweighed my common sense. I figured, "What could possibly happen, besides a big, black mark?" Before any saner thoughts could hinder my progress, I pumped the gun, placed my left hand about five inches from the end of the barrel, and pulled the trigger! I dropped the gun as pain seared through my hand. I surveyed the damage and did not discover the black mark I expected, but there was a small hole in the center of my hand. I began to probe my left hand with my right. I pressed the small hole, and it began to bleed. I was confused until I realized that one little BB had stuck in the chamber and chose to dislodge when my own hand became the target. I tried to squeeze the BB out of my hand like a pimple, thinking it would just pop out if I were to pinch it hard enough. This plan failed and fear began to overtake pain as thoughts of what my mom would do to me began to enter my mind. My conditioning kicked in as I mentally rehearsed every decent lie I thought she might possibly believe.

My top two possible lies were:

1. **I saved my own life.** I had been shooting at the target and heard a BB hit the metal, fence pole. Fearing the BB might have bounced off the pole and be headed toward my eye, I threw my hand up to protect my eye. My instinct proved timely and fortunate when a BB headed directly toward my eye and embedded itself, instead, in my left hand. In this scenario I was a hero with cat-like reflexes who saved his eyesight and possibly his own life. I was like a junior James Bond in training. *Man! This was a good story and almost believable!*

2. **The gun misfired.** I had leaned the gun against the swing set and went to get a drink. When I tried to pick up the gun, I knocked it over. When it fell, it discharged. Luckily, the BB had hit my non-writing and non-throwing hand, so no lasting damage had been done. It was a good story and certainly believable. *But the hero story was much better.*

Planning time was over. It was time to face Mom. Steeling myself for the upcoming confrontation, I walked inside, holding my left hand in my right. Mom stood by the sink and turned to look at me as I entered. Then it hit me that she may have seen the whole thing through the window above the sink. Telling her a lie was just inviting more trouble. I settled for simply telling her the truth.

I said, "Mom, I don't know what I was thinking. I had shot the gun many times and no BB's had come out. Finally, I walked up to the fence and shot it again, and it made a black mark on the target. I thought that was cool and wanted to see if it would leave one on my hand, and . . . well, here are the results." She burst into laughter at the reality that

I had shot myself with a BB gun I'd had for less than an hour. I was momentarily relieved. However, the next thing she said reverberated throughout my body: "I guess we are going to have to go to the hospital and have it taken out." I did not see this coming. I am not really sure what I thought was going to happen, but the hospital? Emergency Room? I was horrified! Five hours and six stitches later, the whole ordeal was over.

The story gets a bit deeper from here forward, as God always has a plan and a lesson to be learned. My stepfather, Larry, worked at the hospital. When it came time to get my stitches out, he had the BB and stitches all placed into the same container. Then, he handed it to me and instructed me to place it on my trophy case. He told me, "The next time you are tempted to shoot yourself, I hope you will take a look at this and have second thoughts." I thought he wanted to make sure I'd learned that I shouldn't play around with any type of gun, since you never know what might happen. A much more profound lesson would hit with great impact only a few months later.

My mother and Larry began to have some marital difficulties. One night when I was spending the night with a neighboring friend, those difficulties led to an explosion of gunfire. Early the next morning, I received a phone call from my mother telling me to come home. When I arrived, mom told me that Larry had put a gun to his head and pulled the trigger. I was in disbelief. Larry had been the first male figure in my life that I thought had it all together. I thought I could learn some things from this guy. I had thought he was different. (This situation serves as another reminder of the dangers of placing all your faith in man rather than God.)

Regardless of the confusion and hurt I felt, there was a lot of clean up to do. It was a mess. My mother had already completed the worst of it, but there were pieces of his hair, teeth, and other Larry-particles stuck in the ceiling. I had to get them out. It was unpleasant, to say the least. As I gathered the gruesome pieces of human carnage, I decided to make a care package for my stepfather and give it to him at the next available opportunity.

Larry had placed a .357 under his chin and pulled the trigger. Because of the angle, the bullet came out the right side of his nasal cavity. It severed his tongue in seventeen places, broke his jaw in three places, and permanently numbed the right side of his face. But he lived.

A few days passed before Mom, Suzanne, and I were able to visit him in the hospital to check on his progress. We all shared pleasantries and tried to sound normal; but he looked bad. I mean the kind of "bad" you look after you shoot yourself in the head. His hair stuck out chaotically, and he had this face-mask-looking, single bar screwed into his jaw. I had never seen anything like this before in my life and haven't seen one since. It was unnerving. It was impossible to ignore, but we didn't want to stare at it. But the harder we tried not to stare, the more impossible it became to look away. I was appalled at how drastically his encounter with a gun had altered him. I tried to refocus on my plan. After spending some quality moments with him, the time came to leave, and I took a small container out of my pocket and handed it to Larry. It contained tiny parts of him I had pried loose from the ceiling. Tears welled in my eyes to a point I could no longer see clearly as I muttered the words, "The next time you want to shoot yourself, I hope you will take a look at this and have second thoughts." I had learned the lesson, but my teacher failed to learn it himself. It was a sad day. I witnessed a man I loved very much make a very bad mistake; he had to live with the consequences for the rest of his life.

The Patch

The patch I earned through this experience and added to my *Trailer Park White Trash* jacket was a **U for unwanted**.

I must admit, looking back upon this time in my life is difficult and confusing. My mother had deemed three men worthy of entering our family; she hoped that each of them, in turn, would be a father to her children. At this age, I trusted my mother's judgement and was optimistic with each new stepfather that things were going to work out; hoping the new husband was truly a good guy. However, as a 13-year-old, I was beginning to question her judgement and believed she needed a better vetting process for the next candidate!

Also, I was beginning to wonder if I was a son that no one wanted. All the men my mom married eventually quit their job of being a dad to Suzanne and me. At some point, you must stop pointing the finger at them and look in the mirror. The thing I most yearned for, the father/son relationship, seemed to be something I would never find. I began having a tough time dealing with the realization. I would lay in bed at night and just look at the ceiling and wonder to God about why I was being denied this relationship I so dearly needed.

I wondered:
Who was going to be my example as a father?
How was I going to learn how to hunt and fish?
Who was going to teach me how to become a husband?

Who was going to teach me how to cut grass, weed eat, and trim the shrubs?

Who was going to teach me how to grill and learn those other outside things?

What had I done wrong?

Was I a horrible kid?

Could I correct whatever made me undesirable?

I so wanted to be the son who had a dad sitting in the ballpark stands bragging about him. Instead, I was the kid being raised by his mother and grandmother. They did their best, but I still needed a dad, in big and small ways. Regardless, at this point in my life, all the potential fathers my mother married did not want to be my dad. In essence, I was unwanted by all the men in my life. I could blame many things; but the bottom line was that no one thought I was worthy of being taught those things all young men expect to learn from their dad.

As a teen, no one was going to feel sorry for me. No one was going to give me four strikes the next time I got into the batter's box. They were not going to give me extra time at school because no male wanted to father me. I know my mother dealt with many of her own issues, but I was an unwanted 13-year-old boy who was desperately in need of help that never came.

There is another side to embracing this patch I have been given. Whether I want the "U" on my letter jacket or not, it's what I received. I have to deal with the consequences of my fatherless situation, be tough enough to accept the circumstances, and work to turn this *Titanic* around. In a world where we always want to blame those around us for our circumstances, often the only growth that happens is in the depth and strength of bitterness and resentment. I realized as life went on that it was critically important for me to look into the mirror and ask myself "What could I do better?" At a young age, I recognized that I needed to refocus my own life and take care of what I could.

I kept this mindset as I grew into a man. But the "U" remained. I still felt unwanted. This did not change until I discovered that I had been loved and wanted all along … by God. At that moment, the "U" was changed to a "W" and firmly affixed to my *Dad Legends* jacket. The "W" stands for wanted. I had to decide I wanted a different life enough to control what I could. And I did. The "W" still stands for wanted, reminding me that I can only control the controllables, but I can focus my wants on things that are achievable. I didn't join the Dad Legends team overnight. But I wanted to be on that team, and by not letting myself get distracted by things out of my control, I was better equipped to get there. And as a dad, I can ensure my children never feel the disappointment of the "U" but can always confidently live in the "W."

The principle I learned most was this:

In life, it's freeing to realize that it is possible to control the controllables but also refuse to beat yourself up over things out of your control.

Huddle Up

Remember, it's our job to prepare and equip the next generation. If you choose to be a dad, then you are choosing to accept the job description that goes along with it. Quitting is not an option. This means you teach your son or daughter right from wrong. You teach them how being loved feels and make sure they feel accepted in their own skin.

Accepting the job and honor of being a dad or a stepdad requires a tremendous amount of energy and dedication. It takes commitment to and sacrifice for your family. There are going to be good times and bad times, but again, quitting is not an option. Your child wants to know that you care about what they think and feel and that you will love them through thick and thin. They need to know that you will never abandon them.

There are some of you reading this who have never, ever thought that your dad might leave you; to you, it seems inconceivable. But there is also a percentage of the world who has never known the feeling of having a dad's arm wrap around them while he tells them, "I love you and you can always depend on me." For me, a big part of changing the "U" to the "W" was realizing that God was my Father, and He is a Father who never leaves His children. He is the Father I can always depend on. He is the Father who teaches me how to be the kind of father I want to be so I can be part of the answer, not the problem.

So can you!

Chapter 4

Fort Lauderdale or Bust

My biological dad, Jerry, arranged for me to work with a man named Pete during spring break of my freshman year of college (1987). Pete was an old friend of my dad from Knoxville who moved to the Miami-Fort Lauderdale area to start his own business and became a fairly successful entrepreneur at the age of 40. At a stout 6-foot-four, Pete was a large and intimidating guy. He lived near Fort Lauderdale, but the flights to Miami were much less expensive. So, to Miami I flew on a non-changeable, non-refundable, and non-transferable round-trip ticket.

All those "nons" didn't seem like a big deal to me at the time. (Boy, was I wrong!) The plan was for Pete to meet me at the Miami airport at 1 p.m., and I would depart for home nine days later at noon. Sounded like a fine plan. Turns out, it was a little lacking in details. I left home as scheduled with $33 in my pocket and caught my connecting flight to Atlanta. We encountered a travel delay, but it didn't even phase me. I was still Miami bound, assuming all would be well.

We finally landed in Miami at around 2:30 and no one met me at the gate, at baggage claim, or in the passenger pick-up area. There were no cell phones, so I sacrificed $2 at the pay phone only to find the phone lines were down between

Miami and Fort Lauderdale. I had assumed my $33 would be plenty for the trip as I would be working for Pete, eating with him, and staying at his condo. But as of this moment, there was no Pete, no job, no transportation, no home address, and no ability to fly back home for nine more days. I was about to be homeless in Miami, Florida.

But what could I do? I relaxed enough to take a nap and woke up starving. I spent another $1 on a snack and wasted a collect call to my dad, who wasn't home. My next dilemma was whether to take the $10 shuttle from the Miami airport to Fort Lauderdale. It would be a $10 sacrifice but at least I could call him, or maybe even remember how to get back to his condo I had visited once in the past. So, I thought I was still fine.

I went for it and arrived in Fort Lauderdale about 10 p.m. I tried numerous times to reach Pete, to no avail. Again, I sat. And sat. Finally, at about 1:30 a.m., I shared my story with an older couple who listened with a bit of empathy. As part of my story, I told them the landmarks I remembered on the way to Pete's condo: a big four-lane highway, a car dealership on the left corner, a bank on the next left. The gentleman looked at his wife and said, "I believe I know exactly where that car dealership is." I could not contain my excitement! After pausing to think for a moment, the gentleman suddenly got an excited look on his face and said, "You know what? I think I know where that condo is." Then I got an excited look on my face and said, "Would you mind taking me there?" A few minutes later, I was in the car with these complete strangers, and we headed toward the condo in Hollywood, Florida. Still doing fine?

Sure enough, he knew where he was going and we found

the place! After telling the gate attendant my story, he felt sorry for me, gave me Pete's condo number and let me in.

I made my way over to Pete's building, but the doors were locked. Of course. It was about 4 a.m., and it had been a very long day, so I laid back on the curb and just tried to relax. I stared at the stars and nearly smiled as I thought back over the strange day. Part of me was shocked and the other part of me was not. I was well aware everything in life does not work out the way you think it will. I had always been a "let's find a way to work this out" kind of person. Quitting was not acceptable. Difficulties weren't dead ends—just speed breakers and hair pin turns. I would just think through the scenarios and come up with possible solutions to overcome hardship and accomplish the task at hand. This trip was no different.

After taking a 15-minute break to count my blessings, I tried to get into Pete's condo building. The doors were still locked, so I continued to wait. About thirty minutes later, an inebriated tenant arrived, and I followed him into the building and made it all the way to Pete's door. I knocked. No one answered and no sound came from inside. So, I went back down to the lobby to plot my next move. Instead, I spotted a couch, laid down and fell asleep. I'm not sure how much time went by before I was awakened by the sound of someone unlocking the lobby doors. Finally, Pete had come home. He looked surprised and said, "Where have you been all afternoon?" I just shook my head and said we'd talk about it tomorrow. I was an exhausted 18-year-old, filled with frustration. No coherent communication was possible at the time. The best thing that could happen was a few hours of sleep before we tackled the next day's events. He helped me with my bags, and we went up to his condo and went to sleep. It was about 5:30 a.m., and I was asleep before the lights went out. I had no idea what the next eight days would bring!

It was time to hit the beach. . . to work. Pete had set up about a dozen food stands on the main drag in Fort Lauderdale. It was a free-for-all on the beach front during the 80's, the wildest spring-break era. I was to work for him every night that week and handle most of the money. During the days, I would just hang out with Pete, ride with him in his white cargo van, and help in whatever ways he needed. The real work started at about 8 or 9 p.m. and lasted until 1 or 2 in the morning. The specific times depended upon the day and the weather.

The strangest thing about this time was that I didn't know Pete at all. I only knew my biological dad was often surrounded by shady business dealings, and it would be wise for me to stay on guard because anything could happen at a moment's notice.

We woke up about noon on Saturday and Pete was on fire to begin his day. I rightly assumed it was a big money day; I was partially right. (The average food stand grossed $3,000–$4,000 per night, which meant Pete's enterprise brought in over $40,000 in one good night. He would gather the cash each night and stuff it into a beat-up briefcase.) He was in an obvious rush, stating he was late for an important meeting, so we needed to get moving. I grabbed some clothes and looked around the condo for something to eat. Finding nothing, I followed Pete to the van. Luckily, I had grown up unaccustomed to three meals every day, so I was ready to go. It was obvious that Pete did not miss many meals, so I knew eating would be on the agenda at some point.

As it turned out, Pete's meeting consisted of the races at the local dog track. All the way there, he talked about quinellas and trifectas, show, place, and win. I had no idea what any of these words meant, but I got a quick education.

By the end of the week, I was becoming an expert! Let me try to describe the process. Pete would place an exorbitant number of detailed bets. Once he had placed all his bets (spending hundreds or thousands of dollars per race), he would watch the race, and immediately following, he would filter through 50–75 betting tickets, pick out the winning ones, cash them in, and do it all over again about fifteen minutes later. Each trip to the betting window (to place wagers or collect winnings) meant a foray into the battered briefcase, filled with a chaotic mess of crumbled, loose currency. I don't believe Pete ever really knew if he ended any day at the track hundreds ahead or thousands poorer. I don't think he cared either way.

After my first experience at the dog track, we took off in the white cargo van and pulled up to a huge warehouse. Inside, were many more vans and tons of workers (all men) who were preparing the food for the night. I mostly just watched and stayed out of the way, trying to look busy. At one point, I took a walk out back. Some of the workers were standing there talking, so I decided to introduce myself. One of the workers, probably in his early 20s, asked me if I had any ice or any rock. Part of me wanted to be cool and say something intelligent to try and fit in but honestly, I had nothing. I did not have the faintest idea of what they were talking about and said as much. To my surprise, the guy said, "You know, crack." I honestly had no earthly idea what he was talking about. More education.

At about 7 that night, we headed out to get set up at our stands. I was assigned to work with a guy nicknamed Hammer

Joe (some names, such as this one, have been changed to protect those involved), and another guy. We operated a stand right outside of the busiest club on the beach. I took orders and collected the money. The other two guys made the food and handed it to the customers. The main thing I remember, after working eight nights with Hammer Joe, is that he was a borderline moron! I wondered how in the world a 40-year-old man possessed zero common sense ... or intelligence. He would do stupid things and mess up the orders; he seemed to have absolutely no memory whatsoever, and certainly no critical-thinking skills. I would berate him carelessly, but he never said a word. He would just mumble under his breath; he was always mumbling.

We went to the dog races whenever possible. Pete would hand me $100 and tell me I had to bet it; if I chose not to, I could watch him gamble. Well, no one learns watching someone else win or lose. The best educator in the world is your own wins and losses (this is also true in life). So, I took my $100 and tried to win, or learn, as much as I could with his money.

The first few times, I lost it all and came back with nothing but an education. The Saturday before I went home was my last chance to visit the dogs. I felt like my luck surely had changed. I was young and naive and just knew *that* day was *my* day. I had lost in every way imaginable throughout the day, including betting on a dog that was disqualified. It was the last race of the evening, and I had just enough money to place a bet on the three dogs I thought would finish first, second, or third. With a little reluctant help from my go-to betting attendant, Sam, I picked my bets and won $500! Not a bad way to end!

I made my flight the next morning and my mom picked me

up at the airport. Compared to my journey nine days before, it seemed a little anticlimactic—until my mom asked me about that trip. I told her I worked one of the Gyro Stands with maybe the dumbest human I had ever met, and I didn't shy away from how I disrespected the guy. Of course, she admonished me and asked his name. She almost wrecked the car when I said Hammer Joe.

Completely freaked out, she looked at me and said, "You know who that is, don't you? Greg, he is a professional hitman; for a specific amount of money, he will wipe you off the face of the earth."

In the face of my shocked expression, she continued: "He will gladly kill you for little to no amount of money. I am shocked your dad didn't tell you he would be down there with you. I am sure your dad arranged for him to work with you, to look out for you."

Like a ton of bricks, I realized that all that mumbling Hammer Joe did was probably a rehearsal of all the ways he could wipe a smug 18-year-old from the earth. Whew. That was a close call and I didn't even know it.

By the way, Pete paid me $550 for working the week and I won $500. Ignoring the first day and remembering the rest, it was a profitable week. Probably the biggest win, considering the people I worked with and my attitude, was that I did not die! For real!

All these years later, my experiences that week are still rather unbelievable. But it happened.

The Patch

The patch I earned through this experience and displayed on

my *Trailer Park White Trash* jacket **was D for dysfunctional.**

As a teenager in this situation, the only thing over which I had control was me. Outside my control were all external facts: I possessed a meager $33 that dwindled quickly; I had no address for my destination; I was stuck in Florida for eight days; and I had no way of contacting the person who failed to meet me at the airport.

The fact that I thrived is a wonder. The whole trip was really doomed from the beginning. I had little direction, guidance, or ability to make solid decisions. The fact that I went down there, survived, and came home with $1,000 is nothing short of a miracle. I was around crime, drugs and no telling what other nefarious activities, and I was practically oblivious to all of it. When placed in the middle of a dangerous situation, I was unprepared and ill-equipped for simple, basic, situational awareness. If this brief examination of the facts does not scream *dysfunction,* then I don't know what would.

I gladly exchanged this "D" patch for a much more hopeful one. My Dad's Legend jacket now sports a "D," but this one stands for Direction. This experience taught me how to think and analyze a situation instead of feeling sorry for myself and being a victim. It taught me to ask questions and work to find solutions that move in the direction of success. In many dire situations, your ability to think on your feet and work toward a successful outcome is critical.

High-level military teams (Seals, Rangers, and others) recognize the fact that decision-making and effective performance in the face of high-pressure events only operate to the level of your training. I believe this is true in sports and in life. Coaches are often judged by their ability (or inability) to make calls in the waning seconds of the half or at the end of the game. The ability to run possible scenarios in their heads as they work through the Rolodex that exists in their minds is imperative. Coaches must search their memories for the situational match to each eventuality and then employ the confidence or guts to make the call. This ability often separates the winners from the losers.

This is true in life. Many people freeze in critical situations or simply refuse to make a decision because they don't want to take responsibility for being wrong. In the end, willingness to make a decision can be the difference between being ultra successful, moderately successful, or unsuccessful. People will make a decision if they are positive their decision will work. Knowing something will work is not the key. Knowing the right direction to head to get closer to your desired destination is the perfect key to every situation. Using your previous experience and situational awareness to help you make an educated guess can often direct your steps ever closer to success.

It is critical to pause and wait for clarity whenever you face a life-changing decision. Determine what result you desire and head off with your eyes fixed in that direction. When on the highway of life, it is very important that you keep your eyes focused out the front windshield and not gazing into the rearview mirror. To live one day looking over your shoulder and not out over the horizon is to rob the value of today! Determine who you want to be and where you want to go; then set a plan in place. Those plans will guide your decision-making and allow you to prosper during the process. It's vitally important that you remember—If you do not know where you are going (in life) any road will take you there! Everyone needs to develop their own internal GPS system.

The principle I want to pass on is:

It's imperative that you have a plan for your life—plan your work and work your plan.

HUDDLE UP

Don't panic when things go awry, because God has wired you to be able to handle those things. I remember hearing a sermon about how the birds don't store up food and yet God provides for them. To truly understand this sermon and what it means that God will provide, you really must have nothing (or no food). If you possess your own food (or whatever you deem is necessary), there is no reason to trust God. When you follow God, you can truly trust in Him and the fact that He cares for your well-being. He will provide. Many times, people have asked me, "Are you not worried about this or that?" and I have responded confidently, "Not in the slightest." This is solely because I do truly believe that God cares about my well-being. My Father in heaven has a plan for my life, and He promised me that He knows my needs and will add all I need to my life . . . if I will seek Him first. (See Matthew 6:33.) Jesus' entire sermon on this subject can be found in Matthew 6:25–34. I promise you it is worth your time to read it and claim it as truth in God's name! He does care about you and your well-being!

Honestly, who can add one minute to their lives or solve any problem by worrying or stressing over? Make educated guesses when you are not absolutely sure and trust the process.

However, this does not mean you can have a lackadaisical view or approach to life. I believe you should bust your butt, prepare, and make the best decision with the facts you have available. Good things just may happen; when they do not, you just get up, dust your pants off, and get back to work!

I am going to ask it one more time for the people in the back. Honestly, who can add one minute to their lives by worrying or stressing over something? Make educated decisions and trust the process. Young Dad, your ability to stay calm and show that you believe in your own decision-making and ability to handle situations that arise does give peace to your wife and children. If every aggressive driver sets you off, do you realize how bad that lack of ability to control your own emotions looks to your kids? If every moron driver sends you into a tizzy and then you spend the next five minutes cussing them and trying to run them off the road (with or without your kids being in the car), what's the point? Always ask yourself if the direction you've chosen is the path you want your children to follow. Control what you can control and let the rest go! Stress, worry, anger—none of these will get you closer to the destination you wish to reach. But God will lead you along a path chosen just for you. Trust Him.

Chapter 5

I'm a Little *What?*

As my senior campaign in high school was winding to a close, it was obvious that I needed some type of scholarship if I had any hope of going to college. And there was a small measure of hope. I did receive some interest from some smaller D1-AA teams, but the only lasting interest that materialized came from Maryville College. The thing that appealed to me most about Maryville College was that they were going to allow me to play football and baseball, so I would basically receive a full scholarship. It was also within 40 minutes of home, and my friend, Sammy, would be playing football there as well. All things considered, it seemed like the right fit. I was about to find out if that was true.

When late July came, Sammy and I moved into our dorm room and began practice with the Maryville College Scots. I was a little nervous and a little excited, without any idea what to expect. I did feel like I had one ace in the hole. Our high school teammate, Jeff, was already on the team, and I believed if push came to shove, he would help us navigate any unseen landmines.

Jeff was part of the defensive backs group, just like me. It was good to have a friend or two on the team, considering my propensity to run my mouth, provoked or not. *(I have seen this be a strength and a weakness in my life.)*

Suffice it to say, the seniors on the team weren't at the top of my friends list. Considering Maryville College was coming off a 3-7 season, there were obviously some leadership issues with the upperclassmen. One result of that was my buddies and I were quickly moving up the depth chart, scoring first or second-string positions, and that was obviously a bit threatening to the players already on the team. The seniors were trying to be leaders, but in ineffective ways. One example was trying to impose their will upon the younger players. For a while, this mainly consisted of yelling at us or having a freshman carry their meal tray—neither effective nor a big enough deal to cause a problem.

However, one day at lunch, things took a turn. All seemed normal until there was a big commotion at the front of the cafeteria. I had hardly been paying attention, but evidently, they were yelling my name. I ignored the yelling. Finally, another player came to inform me I was being summoned. I looked at them said, "I don't care because I am not going up there." This continued for a few more minutes and, to be honest, the room was beginning to get a little tense as they yelled for me, and I did not move.

Eventually, I heard one of them yell, "Stand up!" In response, I stood up and promptly sat right back down. This elicited some snickers throughout the room. Finally, one of the supposed *leaders* of the team came to escort me to the front, where the whole group of supposed *leaders* were huddled to discuss the punishment they were going to bring down upon me for my lack of respect. This punishment? To sing, "I'm a Little Teapot," while acting out the motions. Not having gone to summer camp (because my family summers in the trailer park were more like *survival camp*), I had no idea what they were talking about. But this strong leadership was not to be deterred. They engaged a fourth-string brown-noser who was trying to gain favor with them to show me how it was done.

As he began to sing and act out the motions, I was thinking, "you have got to be kidding me." There is no song that could have sounded sillier or farther from the reality of my life. Meanwhile, the upperclassmen were howling in laughter. Then, it was my turn. I had zero desire to do this, but I also did not know what would happen to me if I did not comply. So, I swallowed my pride and began the song and dance. Bending my knees to mimic the other guy, I declared "I'm a little teapot, short and stout." Some of the players laughed, some booed, and some just sat in shock. Needing to prove a point and put me in my place, the senior stopped me and demanded I start again, with more energy and volume. Trying to comply and get this embarrassment over with, I started again. "I'm a little Teapot, short and stout, here is my…" That's as far as I got. My nemesis stepped in to berate me about how bad I was and how he could not believe I did not know this song. He then said, "Where have you been living, under a rock?"

It sounds like a harmless statement, but it struck a nerve. Here's why. Even though I grew up in the trailer and faced plenty of hard times, I always believed I maintained my basic dignity and self-esteem. Not so here in the lunchroom. What was taking place was embarrassing the fool out of me in front of the whole team and, I was not handling it well. As this moment dragged on, my willingness to comply was reaching its limits, and the TP kid with limited social grace was about to come bubbling to the surface.

As they laughed, yelled, and told me to begin again, I turned to the leader with newfound strength and said, "Bleep You and I am not doing another thing. If this is how you lead this team, no wonder you went 3–7 last year! Bleep off." With that, I began my exit. The problem was, I had to walk past all the coaches as I exited the facility. And I was disappointed with every coach there. I was in shock they simply sat and watched this instead of stepping in to provide a healthy and safe environment for all their players. How I handled it may not have been my best moment. Once again, that saying ("You can take the kid out of the Trailer Park but not the Trailer Park out of the kid") was holding true. I stopped at the coaches' table and confronted the head coach. "If this is how you are going to run a program, then I don't want to have anything to do with it."

With that, I walked out of the building and off the team. I tucked my tail and ran home to the comfort of my mother and girlfriend. I quit my dream of playing college sports because some small-minded wannabe leader tried to make me look silly. You know, I must not have been too committed to that dream to allow it to be thrown away that quickly. I was still able to attend college, however. My mother had begun working at the University of Tennessee, so I could attend school there tuition-free. That's what I did.

I was a freshman in college with nothing and no one to keep me accountable and responsible. No teammates or coaches keeping tabs on me and checking on my well-being. I was a ship without a rudder in the ocean of life. I had zero direction and guidance. I went to class when I wanted to, skipped when I felt like it, and didn't care much about academic success. But something began to change. I decided I was tired of starving to death and wanted to major in business administration. I was sure that would help me become a millionaire!

That first semester I remember attending an economics class. I could barely understand the teaching assistant, and I only spoke broken econ, so I was lost. It had disaster written all over it. I did not know you could drop a class after so many weeks, so I just sat in there and drowned with a C or D. Making that million wasn't looking so good.

I struggled through the rest of the year and all three quarters at UT. It had nothing to do with the academic rigor but rather with my focus and desire to be successful. School at this point meant nothing to me and, again, I was floating in a world of mediocrity and didn't care enough about anything to want to succeed.

I reached the midpoint of the third quarter after Spring break (my infamous week in Fort Lauderdale). I decided I would finish this quarter, but after that I was finished with college and was going to get a job. After all, there are millions of examples of people who did not go to college but ended up making a very good living. Why couldn't I be one of those people?

As summer approached, I needed to find my entry point into the marketplace, as I was about to be well on my way to millions of dollars. I mean, if Nike can be sold out of the trunk of a car in the beginning and Apple was started in a garage, then why could not I be a pioneer in something? So . . . how was I going to change the world? I began to look at the want ads, and it did not take me too long to realize that they sure did not want me. I was looking at the qualifications for a lot of those jobs, and I noticed that not one of them started out with:

Looking for College drop-out, little to no experience needed, history of quitting anything hard or tough.

Yeah, I began to doubt the hypothesis I had sold myself this past three to five months. However, I had to try. Going back through the want ads, I came across this ad that stated

Wanted: Salesmen to provide educational demonstrations, no experience necessary as we will train all our salesmen, $8-16 an hour.

It should have said something like this:

Send us your lame, sick and faking: we will send them out on a hopeless adventure. And after spending a few days with us, if they are not ready to go back to school, then there is nothing in the world that can motivate them, except maybe ditch digging.

I read it and thought, "Bingo, I am in! Might be the only ad I even remotely qualify for, so here goes." I called the number and accepted an interview time. I did not even know what product I would be selling, but whatever it was, at $8-16/hour, I was in! After a quick 30-minute meeting, they deemed me worthy. I would begin demonstrating the latest greatest, "aerosol-sized fire extinguisher." I admit I was skeptical, but once I heard their sales pitch, I was convinced everyone needed one of these marvels. People make money in all kinds of different ways. Some sell beer and carbonated drinks to stores. Some invent things and make millions of dollars. At the time, I thought I was about to go buck wild and be a selling fiend. I would probably set some company records on the way, and money was going to be pouring in before long. I would finally be well on my way to my first million. Well, I was wrong.

I had made some calls over the weekend and lined up a few demonstrations that, of course, would turn into sales. I called every one of my friends' parents and asked them if I could drop by their place of business or home and show them a quick presentation that could potentially be lifesaving. Many signed up and I was on my way. One day after another I gave demonstrations. Sales were not racking up. My professional career was almost nonexistent. And my personal life? My high school sweetheart called and let me know that I was being put on waivers (aka she wanted to be single during her senior year). Really, I think the deciding scenario played out in her home and went something like this:

Denise's parents: "Hey Denise, your boyfriend came by today and told us about his new career path. Well, we can do this one of two ways. Either you can call him and make up some lame excuse to break up, or we can call him and tell him the truth about what a loser he has become."

Denise: "Hey Greg. I want to be single my senior year of high school."

Yeah, that's really what I believe transpired, and she gave me the easy way out. Life could not have been any worse for me at that time, and it was all 100 percent my fault. The breakup shocked me back to reality, and I took a good hard look at my life. I looked at the guy staring back at me in the mirror and thought, "I really am a loser!" I sat at the kitchen table facing reality. My mom was at work, and my girlfriend gave me the pink slip, so it was just me. I knew I needed to make a real change. What could I do? What really mattered to me?

The only thing I could think of was playing college football again.

Was there anyone in my life who would care enough to share some solid advice with me? I decided to call Coach Kerry, my old high school football coach. As we talked, he told me one of my high school teammates was going down to play football at Tennessee Wesleyan University. They were just starting a football program, and it would be a good opportunity to play immediately. I said, "where and who?" I thought I knew a lot of the schools around our area, but I had never heard of that one.

I got in touch with Coach Bankston at TWU. After a conversation, he asked me to pick up an unofficial transcript from UT and bring it to meet him at 11 a.m. the next day. I was so excited, I could barely sleep the night before. That morning, I picked up my transcript and dropped off my fire extinguisher demo kit before arriving in Athens, Tennessee, right on time. Coach and I walked over to the school registrar, who had the ability to make or break my future. I wanted to make a positive impression. Slight hitch in that plan was the fact I was one hour short of qualifying. I gave her my best smile and asked if there was anything she could do to help me.

I briefly explained my current situation and promised that if she helped me get eligible, I would graduate in four years, and I would be the poster child for accomplishment. God must have intervened at that moment because she found a way for me to get a one-hour bowling credit. I gave her the biggest smile of my life and thanked her profusely. But she wasn't done with me. I had to declare a major. I thought about the way Coach Kerry had, in the past 24 hours, literally helped change the course of my life. I told her, "I want to be a teacher." However, we were still not done. I had to pick a subject and couldn't choose PE. I chose social studies. That day set me on a course to where I am today. I wasn't a little teapot. I wasn't a fire extinguisher salesman. I wasn't a quitter. I was a football player. I was going to be a social studies teacher.

THE PATCH

The letter jacket patch I earned from this experience for my *Trailer Park White Trash* jacket was a **DR for Dirt Road**.

The *Dirt Road* exemplifies a tougher way of life. You believe you are not worthy of the easy way. If you are given the easy route, you probably will not appreciate nor learn from it. Sometimes you must go through some tough times, be at the end of your rope, and realize you have nowhere to go but up. You also know that quitting is not an option, and you have no choice but to get up off the mat, *one more time*, and answer the bell. This is what the *Dirt Road* of life means. It means you don't expect anything to be easy as nothing has ever been easy. You have no reason to believe it will change now.

My friend, Theron, and I used to stand at practice and talk about how many lessons you learn traveling that *Dirt Road*. It's like the rich kids who got everything they ever wanted, from a new car to the newest shoes, and don't appreciate what they have. It's so easy to take everything for granted. Contrast that with the kids who had to get a job and save their money for their vehicle. How many times do you see the spoiled kid's car filthy? Probably a lot. But the kid who bought and paid for his 20-year-old, outdated car has kept it clean, inside and out. This is the *Dirt Road*. It's hard and it's not always fair, but if you are tough enough and keep answering that proverbial bell, then you have a chance to make it.

Life on the *Dirt Road* can be messy. You may have made a bad decision, and that *Dirt Road* turned into a muddy mess. Well, this just gives you another opportunity to prove to yourself how tough you are! See, you must convince *yourself* that you are worth fighting for. You have been given the chance to be a dad when so many others have not or will not join the team. Being a good dad is worth fighting for. Also, when the road gets muddy, you will find out who your real friends are, who really cares about your well-being. Basically, you'll find out who is in your circle. It matters.

I actually transferred the DR patch to my *Dad Legends* jacket because I still find so much value in the *Dirt Road*. Especially as a dad, I don't ever want to take my journey for granted. And I want to encourage my children to learn from their journeys as well. Things won't ever be perfect. Challenges won't ever cease. But that's good because they can motivate us to keep moving.

Traveling the *Dirt Road* does not mean you will succeed, but it does mean that you will get a chance if you keep getting up every time you get knocked down. It's all about getting another chance to prove you are worthy of whatever it is you are trying to accomplish. Sometimes you get up and reach that goal, and sometimes you get to learn that lesson all over again. Obviously, you want to minimize those relearned opportunities! However, this too is life. Stop screaming about Rule Number1 (life is not fair), and start developing your own internal beast that wants to prove to all those doubters and haters in the world that you really can do it! The devil would not be attacking you so hard if there was not something valuable in you! Remember, thieves do not break into an empty house.

The principle here that I want to share with you is:
Embrace the Dirt Road of life Philosophy. Stand up, dust off your pants, and get busy walking towards your goals.

HUDDLE UP

When accepting the responsibilities of being a dad, you must embrace everything that comes with it. Your children did not choose you. They did not choose their circumstances. They do not want to hear about your hardships or how tough you had it. They want to know can they count on you, that you will meet their basic needs, and you will do more than the average dad.

That *Dirt Road* of life just helps you create a mentality that recognizes life is tough, and you don't need to waste your time looking for the shortcut because it does not exist. You don't even waste your time believing in the *lottery philosophy* of life. What is the *lottery philosophy* of life, you ask? Why do people spend countless dollars on scratch-off tickets and the Mega Millions? They play it because they believe they can pay one, two, or three dollars and they will receive $500 million. That is the *lottery philosophy*. The only problem is that you are most likely not going to win. That is the reality with the lottery and in life. People believe that, at some magical point, a person is going to pay all their bills or give them a new car for no reason at all. When these things do not happen, they spend their time complaining about how life is not fair, and they can never get a break. Well, with the *Dirt Road* of life philosophy, you have already accepted that no one is going to walk up and give you a million dollars. Instead, your motto is: if it's to be, it's up to me. You know, at the beginning of each and every day, the only person you can count on will meet you in the mirror when you brush your teeth, and it's that guy who will follow you around every day, believing you can do it!

As a dad, it's your job to raise tough-minded and hard-working kids. We (their mom and I) decided early on that we did not want our children to get a new car at age 16. So, we decided that whatever money they had saved by 16, we would match it. As a result, if they had worked and saved $4,000, then it would be $8,000 total for a car. We would take that amount and buy the best vehicle available at the time. We believed if they had skin in the game (their own money), that they would do a better job of taking care of the vehicle, and it would mean more to them. We also believed that if we just bought them a new car, they would not really appreciate it as much as they would when they were able to buy their own new car. This may not be the exact route for everyone, but it has held true and worked for us and our *Dirt Road* philosophy.

CHAPTER 6

BRENNAN McCOOL

I began teaching at Christian Life Academy in 1992. I was a young, clueless, upbeat ball of piss and vinegar, as they say; full of life, but at times short on common sense. I finished my master's degree at Tennessee Tech University, working as a graduate assistant football coach and student. I then accepted a coaching and teaching position at this small private school in Louisiana. I figured this was far enough away from Tennessee that if I was not a very good coach, no one back home would find out. And maybe, when I decided to go back home, I could tell my own story.

I taught PE to the seventh–twelfth graders and coached football and baseball. We were your typical private school that had sprung up in Louisiana as the public schools began to fail and deteriorate. Our school was a K-12 Christian school with an evangelical approach to education. This meant that, in a world where no one is perfect, we did not require our students to already be Christians upon entering the school. However, students and parents agreed to abide by the rules and requirements of the school. Also, our school followed a traditional six-period day; I taught five of the six periods.

My first class after lunch, fifth period, was a general PE course. We played games like whiffle ball, kick ball, football, soccer, and basketball, changing sports about every three weeks. In this fifth-period class, I met a freshman young man who was mad at the world, although I had no idea why. It's easy to pick out those angry students as it's typically written all over their faces, day after day. Well, that attitude typically did not phase me as I was prepared to play five periods of whatever was on the agenda for the day. I was excited because at 24 years old, I thought, "What could make our PE classes better than if I was all-time QB during the football games or all-time pitcher during whiffle ball?" Seriously, I had the degree in PE, so who was the expert here, right?

In a PE class, we typically have 30-40 students, and it usually takes a few weeks to learn all their names. But it only took me about two or three days to learn the name Brennan McCool as he was constantly throwing the ball at someone when things did not go his way. If he was not doing something to get my attention, then this young, small, athletic player would begin to gripe and complain about everything we did.

Since this was my first year of teaching, I was a bit unprepared. I know it's hard to believe, but when you're getting your education in college, they never teach you about ways to handle classroom management. It might be the first thing you need to learn when dealing with children: how to keep class going without allowing distractions from that group of students who don't want to participate or who need extra attention to stay on task. Brennan was constantly vying for my attention, and not the good kind of attention either. He would be pestering someone or flipping someone a bird or cussing when he made a bad play. I thought back to high school and what my PE teacher, Mrs. Julian, would do in similar situations. She would just tell us to run a lap. According to that logic, you would think Brennan was trying out for the cross-country team based upon how much he would run during a given class period. No sooner than he would finish one lap, he would act out again and be on his way around the football or baseball field for another lap.

The one thing I noticed about Brennan was that he was never disrespectful, but he just needed attention and did not know how to control his emotions. He would make me laugh most of the time. For instance, after a few weeks of this acting out and running laps cycle, he would have one of his patented insane responses to a mistake he had made and without me saying anything, he would just start running.

One day, I asked the youth pastor at CLA, Pat Hymel, to share Brennan's story with me. (Pat usually knew the story of most of the students.) He began to explain to me that Brennan's parents were divorced, and Brennan had been living with his mom in Florida, where he began going down a personally destructive path. If my memory serves me right, I believe he was a little bit of a handful, and his mom was not a very strong disciplinarian, so she threw her hands up in defeat. As a result, both parents agreed that he needed to move to Baton Rouge and live with his dad, the sterner disciplinarian.

In life, I do believe it is very important to listen to someone's story, when possible, as it always helps you better understand where they are coming from and, possibly, why they act the way they do. Ultimately, Brennan was upset about moving to Baton Rouge and was lashing out with his behavior and negative reactions to things that were happening in class. That behavior actually had nothing to do with PE but was more about his frustration over his current situation. Also, his dad was laying down the hammer at home, which was upsetting to him as well. I now had a much better picture of who Brennan McCool was. I knew at one point in my own life I needed a coach to step in, with a positive influence. I thought if I could help Brennan, it would be worth it. Now, understanding the picture a little better, I began to have a few more one-on-one conversations with him, when time allowed.

As the semester progressed, Brennan's lap running desire did not change much, but he was beginning to warm up to me. We were fast approaching Thanksgiving Break, and Brennan announced to the class that he was going to try out for the baseball team. Everyone started laughing, but none more than me. I was the head baseball coach. I thought, "There is no way I am going to allow him on the baseball team." Once he announced that he was going to try out, the entire class looked at me for my response. I just smiled and said, "No Way!"

As class was winding down and we began to walk off the field, Brennan rushed up to me and said, "Coach, I am serious. I played baseball in Florida before I moved here."

Turning to look at Brennan, I replied, "Brennan, I work every day teaching whomever goes to school here from 8 to 3, but I have a say in who I am around from 3 to 8. If you think I am going to be around you and the way you act from 3 to 8, you are greatly mistaken."

He said, "Coach, I won't act like that during baseball practice."

I then said, "Brennan, I tell you what I will do. If you can go from Thanksgiving break to Christmas break without getting into trouble in PE class, I will allow you to come out. However, this does not mean I am going to allow you on the team. But I will allow you to try out. What do you think about that?"

Brennan said, "Are you serious coach? I promise you won't be disappointed!" He literally skipped off with excitement.

As he ran off, I remember thinking, "There is no way Brennan can go three weeks without getting into trouble. His track record has shown that he gets into trouble two or three times a period. No chance he makes it."

The most bizarre thing took place over the next three weeks. Much to my amazement, Brennan became a model student. I was in shock; the class clown had become one of the best students in the class. It brought a smile to my face. As Christmas break quickly approached, McCool came up to me and asked, "Coach, have I behaved enough to where I can try out for the baseball team?" Smiling at him, I said, "You know what Brennan, you sure have. I just hope you can hit a baseball now." I had learned a valuable lesson already, early into my teaching and coaching career. Once someone has purpose and focus, it can change his or her life. I now just hoped McCool could play a little so that I would have a reason to put him on the team.

Tryouts were the first two weeks of 1993 and sure enough, Brennan showed up for tryouts. He was a scrappy little five-foot-6, 135-pound outfielder who had good speed and worked hard. At this time in his career, he was not outstanding, but he was definitely good enough to make the JV baseball team. At the end of two weeks, Brennan found himself on the list of players making the team.

He had a solid freshman season, nothing too outstanding and nothing too bad either. The biggest change was in my class. He was still in my fifth-period class, but instead of messing around and getting into trouble he was now a model citizen. Brennan had completely changed his attitude and effort all because he found himself being part of a bigger machine—he had joined a team and become a teammate in the process.

Brennan's first year at CLA, he had only played baseball, but that summer and fall he had decided to join the football team. I was thrilled as the defensive backs coach and defensive coordinator on the football team. McCool would naturally be a defensive back or wide receiver as that's where all the 5-foot-8 white kids find themselves in the football world. Come on over, Brennan, and just cozy on up to your new reality. As a 5-foot-8 wide receiver, he would be forced to block defensive backs a lot bigger than himself. At defensive back, he would be forced to cover wide receivers a lot bigger than himself. So, in essence, he would be facing an uphill battle to play as a sophomore on the varsity but was set to have a great JV season. These harsh realities did not faze him, and he just showed up every day ready to work, exactly like he had once he made the baseball team.

Spring rolled around and once again McCool tried out for the baseball team and made it. He also became our starting centerfielder that year and usually hit second in the lineup. We had a solid team, and Brennan led the team in stolen bases. He was a highly competitive player, and winning was high on his priority list. I remember a game against Parkview Baptist, a team that had been a perennial powerhouse in Baton Rouge for a few years. We were facing one of their ace pitchers, and it was a tight game. Their pitcher had been quick pitching us, and we were constantly calling time to disrupt his rhythm.

The other coach was constantly objecting to that. Also, when no one was on base, this pitcher had been almost untouchable. Brennan was leading off the inning, and I called him down to the third base coaches' box to talk to him before he went up to bat. While we were talking, I asked McCool to look at how the catcher was extending his hand too close into the bat path. I pointed out that if he would slightly extend his bat back through his swing path then he could get catcher's interference and get on first base. He looked at me and asked, "What do you want me to do?" I said, "Brennan, just extend your bat a little as you attempt to hit the ball and see if you hit his glove, as we need some base runners." He said, "You got it coach."

Brennan stepped into the batter's box and took strike one right down the middle. I thought, "Are you kidding me?" I wanted to give him some type of signal to extend his hands and hit the catcher's glove, but I wasn't sure how I could do that without giving away what we were about to do. So, I just looked at Brennan and said, "Come on, you got this." I hoped he did what I asked him to do. Next pitch resulted in a ball and the count was 1-1. Here came another pitch—another ball. The count was now 2-1. I just stayed the path and clapped and told Brennan, "There's nobody better." I figured he would have to throw one over the plate on this pitch, so here we went. Sure enough, the pitcher rocked, pivoted, and threw the ball right over the plate. McCool started his swing but instead of slightly extending his hands to hit the catcher's glove, he extended his arms and smacked the catcher's mask right off his face! The umpire declared catcher's interference as McCool ran to first base. Their coach came screaming out of the dugout yelling, "He did that on purpose!" Being only

25 at this time, I was not skilled in the art of deception and had to turn and look into left field to keep from laughing, as this had turned into a comedy routine. Brennan was making his way to first base while also trying to act like he was concerned and shocked that he had made contact with the catcher. I eventually walked down to home plate and stressed that there was no way our player would do something like that and told their coach he was crazy for thinking such a thing. After all, we were from a Christian school! He calmed down and went back into the dugout. This is just one of the stories I remember about Brennan and his willingness to do whatever was best for the team and of course, to win.

We went on to make the playoffs for the first time in school history. I am not sure who we were playing, but we had to travel to New Orleans to play them. The fact that we had made the playoffs was nothing short of a miracle considering this team was 0-20 two years earlier (I was not the coach at that time). They were the higher seed, so we had to drive down to play them, as the visiting team. Everyone on the team was excited and could not wait to represent the school in the playoffs. The players were in their uniforms but with tennis shoes or turf cleats on, as cleats were not allowed on the bus. Arriving at the game site a few hours before game time, our players piled off the bus to warm up and hit. Naturally, upon arrival they would change shoes, go to the bathroom, and make their final preparations for hitting and throwing. As this is going on, I noticed that Brennan was in a small but visible panic. He was going back to the bus, looking under the seats, looking in his bag . . . something was amiss. As I walked over to him, I noticed one of the back-up players taking their cleats off and Brennan putting them on.

I asked, "What's going on?"

The other player said, "Brennan forgot his cleats, and I am giving him mine."

I said, "No, that's not what is going to happen. Murray did not forget his cleats, and it's not fair for him to not be able to play. So you are going to sit out, not him."

Brennan went nuts. "That's not fair. I have worked all season to be able to start this game. He is not as good as I am, and I am more important to the team."

I answered. "All of that is true, but the bottom line is, you forgot your cleats and are not prepared to play. He did not. You are not playing."

Let's just say the next few minutes were bad for Brennan as he came to grips with the reality that he was not going to be part of the first baseball playoff game in CLA history. His role was going to be to support his teammates to the best of his ability by cheering for them and encouraging them during the game.

The game could not have gone much better for the Crusaders as we hit four or five home runs during the game and run-ruled our opponent. We handily won our first-round playoff game and were set to play again the next week, at home. The players were beside themselves with excitement and energy. That is everyone except Brennan McCool. I noticed that every time we hit a home run, everyone would sprint out of the dugout to celebrate the hit and congratulate their teammate, except one selfish player. He had refused to celebrate or be excited about what was happening. He was so busy wallowing in his own self-pity that he could not see the silver lining that was transpiring (he would get to play a second-round playoff game).

After the game ended, I pulled Brennan aside for a quick conversation. I asked him, "Why didn't you celebrate those home runs with your teammates? Did you not realize that if we win this game, you will get to play in the next one? How can you be so short-sighted that you do not realize our success today allows you to redeem yourself in the next game? You were so busy feeling sorry for yourself that you missed the blessing of the victory. I am tremendously disappointed. You proved today that you are only for the team when you are one of the starters. But when you are not starting, then it's all about Brennan. That, in itself, is disappointing. Brennan, here is where I am after watching you today. I am going to give you till practice tomorrow to decide if you want to be part of this team or not. If you want to remain on the team, at the beginning of practice I need you to apologize to the entire team for being so selfish. If you will apologize to them and they accept it, you and I will have some quality time at the end of practice to try and ensure that you remember why you may want to always choose to be a teammate over being an individual."

The next day at practice, after we had warmed up and were about to transition into fundamentals, Brennan asked if he could talk to the team for a second. Of course I obliged him. Once all the players came up and took a knee, he told them how sorry he was for how he had acted; he was embarrassed for letting them down and that was not the type of teammate he wanted to be. All was forgiven, and we continued practice. Brennan had learned a valuable lesson about team and the individual's role within that team. We won the next round, and Brennan started and played solidly as he most always did.

Baseball season ended, and Brennan rolled right into

summer workouts and football. He started at cornerback this next season (his junior year). Remember, I was the secondary coach, and he played the position I coached, so again he was under my tutelage during the entire season and accountable to me for his play on the field. He was a small 5-foot-8 corner that played 6-foot. He competed and was scrappy on the field. His desire to be good and be accountable to his teammates kept him in the lineup. Many times, he would go up against players bigger than he was, but he would not back down. When they threw passes to the person he was guarding, he would tackle them, knock the ball out of their hands or just stop them. He had a solid season, and we eventually lost in the semi-finals and ended our year with the best record in school history at 13-1.

So, as you can see, Brennan and I spent a ton of time together, but there was even more he was doing to spend time with me. As the head baseball coach, I sold doughnuts every morning to raise money for the baseball program. I would stop by the grocery store and pick up five to six dozen glazed circles of happiness, and we would sell them before school from 7:45 to 8:05 in the cafeteria. Well, Brennan had volunteered to help me sell them and, almost every day, he would be there to help me. So, from his sophomore season up until now, Brennan and I sat together and just talked about anything and everything every morning. This young man who was lost and without direction had become my little brother as there were only about eight to ten years difference between us. He had grown on me, and I trusted him completely with the money for the program and every other aspect of our program, as well.

Since he helped me sell doughnuts almost every morning,

he called me one Thursday evening to tell me that he would not be able to help me Friday morning. He was going to go by and pick up one of his friends on the way to school and thus, he would not get to school until about 8 a.m. I told him not to worry about it and that I would take care of the doughnut sales.

Friday morning was just like every other morning. I arrived at school about 7:40 and sold doughnuts until about 8:05, or until I ran out. Then, I went to my office to get ready for first period. At about 8:15, the youth pastor came to my office. I imagined he just stopped by to say hello or hang out for a few minutes as we were really close friends. However, that was not the case this Friday morning. He said that there had been a wreck on the way to school that involved Brennan. Naturally, I asked him if McCool was okay, and he looked at me and dropped his head and said, "No." I said, "What are you talking about?" He then told me that Brennan had been killed in a one-car accident on the way to school. I really cannot even begin to tell you the emotion that overtook me at that time. I had always been emotionally calm when it came to tragedy or crisis. But this time, I completely lost it. I began to cry as my heart broke on the spot for this kid and his family. After a few minutes, I asked the administration if I could drive out to his parents' house to just try and console them for their loss. I really had no idea what to do, as this was uncharted water for me. I don't remember them telling me how to handle something like this in the coaching or teaching manual.

Pat and I jumped into the car and drove out to Brennan's home. Driving in silence the entire way, the 20-minute ride seemed like five minutes as I sat there numb. We pulled into a sea of vehicles as family members and friends had shown up to do the same. I remember hugging his dad and stepmom at great lengths as all we could do was hug and cry. There were no words for this moment, as a beautiful soul had been taken much too early for any of us to try to understand. I remember walking into his room where his Bible was open on his desk because he had been working on his morning devotional before school.

Over the next three days, I cried at great lengths. Every time I thought about this young man and how he had completely changed his own life in those short two and a half years, I broke down and cried. I had many conversations with God about why He would allow this to happen. I asked God those crazy questions that all of us think about but never want to admit. I am talking about questions like, "God, why didn't you take that kid in my third-period class who cares about no one and hates life? That kid is never going to make a difference. But Brennan was on a road that led him to not only change his life, but he was going to change the lives of others around him." It sounds harsh, but those are the spur-of-the-moment, emotionally-charged questions that bubble out in such a devastating moment. I cried about the potential for a great human that had been stolen. That song by Billie Joel had never rung truer, "Only the Good Die Young." This young man's life had been ripped from all of us close to him, and I was having a tough time dealing with it and understanding how it could be part of God's plan. It's still difficult to understand.

THE PATCH

The letter jacket patch I earned from this experience that

could have fit on the *Trailer Park White Trash* jacket was a L for Loner. Feeling alone, like he was an island, was not a positive or healthy thing for Brennan. It helped him stay in a place of anger and negative attention-seeking. I know I can relate to that. Can't you? When you feel like you're the odd one out, you often go ahead and act out. If you don't belong, might as well make it uncomfortable for everyone. We see this often in children, but it can also follow us into our adult lives.

Knowing that, because of Christ we do fully belong, is life changing. We belong to Him, to His family, forever. And we have a world of Christian brothers and sister to walk through life with, however long that time may be.

For my *Dad Legends* letter jacket, I switched the **L** patch to a **T for Team.**

Brennan McCool confirmed something that I had always believed. Becoming part of a team can change your life.

So, looking back on it, when Brennan forgot his cleats, it probably hurt me worse than it hurt him. I hated to break his heart and tell him he was not going to play. I had to discipline him for his mistake, yet no part of me wanted to do so. However, if he was going to learn accountability and responsibility, then he needed to receive the discipline of the coach. That is what I had signed up for, to be their coach and all that came with it. I could not be their coach when things went well only to abandon them, refusing the responsibility, when we were losing, and things were not going well. I was learning some valuable lessons about leadership and accountability.

I mentioned it earlier, but I want to stress it again. McCool found himself part of something bigger than himself—a team. When you join a team, you are freely choosing to adhere to its rules and requirements. You learn hard work and sacrifice as well as punctuality, accountability, and the need for a positive attitude. Brennan was falling right into line and was doing all these things. He loved baseball, but more than that, he had found a home on the team and in the commitment to be a good teammate. People who never played team sports really do not understand this. There are so many lessons learned in team sports that cannot be taught in the classroom or at home. Through Brennan McCool, I learned this lesson again, early on in my career, and I want to thank him for showing me that all types of kids can be good teammates. It's not just the best players with the best attitudes, but it is also the tough-to-coach kid who probably needs the team more than the team needs him.

Together
Everyone
Achieves
More

Ultimately, realizing that your individual decisions hurt the team can change a person's behavior. It is that transformation that each man needs to realize when he starts thinking about forming a family.

Once you choose to start your own team, you need to realize that you are now the Owner, Chief Financial Officer and Head Coach. Everyone on the team looks to you for direction and guidance. All great companies are founded on leadership and that is no different in a family. Dad, your desire to meet their needs and provide for them helps every one of them enjoy the stability of a healthy growing environment.

The Principle I want to share is as follows:

Dad, once you start your own team, you accept the responsibilities of being the Owner, CFO and Head Coach.

HUDDLE UP

Although I was the coach and he was the student, Brennan McCool taught me several things that I apply in my life today. The number one lesson is love! I never wanted one of my children to not know what my love for them looked like. My love for them has no end. I wanted them to know what a genuine hug given with love felt like. Too many men do not lean in and hug their children without getting stiff or feeling "funny." That is a shame! Every child wants to run into the arms of its dad and just be consumed with his hug. It is that feeling (the all-consuming hug from dad) I hope I experienced as a child, but I cannot remember it, if I did. However, I want all my children today to know what a hug feels like, at every age and stage of development.

Losing Brennan McCool made me realize how precious life really is and that all of us are never guaranteed tomorrow. It made me want to ensure that everyone I cared about in my life, from other men to my family members, knew that I loved them, and I cared for them. I never wanted to hide a hug or my love from them. Life is too short to stay mad and to hide your love. You will never regret loving your children by telling them but also showing them with a hug! It's equally true with your *bro* friends! Many men do not know what love is. It's a shame! Love the people who matter to you! Love them without end. Love them like they are your family members. Wives are a blessing, and I'm sure grateful for mine! Sometimes, though, you need other like-minded male friends in your life as well. Seek out positive ones and add them to your "family." Also, remember what family means.

Forget
About
Me
I
Love
You

CHAPTER 7

So, If I Lie to the Pastor...

It was my fourth year at Christian Life Academy, and we were beginning to have a lot of success athletically in football and baseball. We had just finished our second consecutive 13–1 football season, and things were going well. I was about to start my fourth season as the head baseball coach. We were also coming off our best baseball season ever at 25–5 and had a lot of players coming back. During the fall, the founder of the school decided to build an extension onto the school. In pursuit of this extension, the home dugout for our baseball team was demolished. Of course, this happened with the intention of having it rebuilt before the season started.

Well... the middle of February came, and the home dugout still had not been rebuilt. I was young and believed there was no use worrying about it as there was nothing I could do. There was only one person who could correct this wrong, and it was the founder. A few years before, a parent had donated his time, resources, and energy building the dugouts, so I was out of favors to try to get it rebuilt on my own.

At CLA, the faculty and staff had prayer every Wednesday morning. We would all show up about 7:30, someone would speak for a few minutes, and then we would pray and be dismissed. One particular morning, the founder was speaking, and he shared this passage from the Bible, about forgiveness:

Then Peter came up and said to Him, "Lord, how many times shall my brother sin against me and I still forgive him? Up to seven times?" Jesus said to him, "I do not say to you, up to seven times, but up to seventy-seven times.

"For this reason the kingdom of heaven is like a king who wanted to settle accounts with his slaves. And when he had begun to settle them, one who owed him ten thousand talents was brought to him. But since he did not have the means to repay, his master commanded that he be sold, along with his wife and children and all that he had, and repayment be made. So the slave fell to the ground and prostrated himself before him, saying, 'Have patience with me and I will repay you everything.' And the master of that slave felt compassion, and he released him and forgave him the debt. But that slave went out and found one of his fellow slaves who owed him a hundred denarii; and he seized him and began to choke him, saying, 'Pay back what you owe!' So his fellow slave fell to the ground and began to plead with him, saying, 'Have patience with me and I will repay you.' But he was unwilling, and went and threw him in prison until he would pay back what was owed. So when his fellow slaves saw what had happened, they were deeply grieved and came and reported to their master all that had happened. Then summoning him, his master *said to him, 'You wicked slave, I forgave you all that debt because you pleaded with me. Should you not also have had mercy

on your fellow slave, in the same way that I had mercy on you?' And his master, moved with anger, handed him over to the torturers until he would repay all that was owed him. My heavenly Father will also do the same to you, if each of you does not forgive his brother from your heart."

~Matthew 18:21–35 NASB

We prayed and were dismissed.

It was the time of year when we would get packages for the baseball team. I would pick them up in the school office and then drive them over to my office to be put up till needed. This was the second season we had a golf cart that we used to drag the field and to carry things around the campus. It had served us well and was a nice gift from one of the parents.

On Thursday night, about 8 or 8:30, I was still at school. I had grabbed a few boxes from the school office and was heading back to the gym to drop them off. I had more boxes than normal this evening, but I had traveled this route many times and could do it in my sleep. As I was traveling down the front of the church and past the building's columns, the number of boxes I had on the cart was making maneuvering more challenging than normal. I slowed down to ensure that I did not hit the building, but the boxes inhibited my view of the bottom right of the golf cart and I nicked the column as I went by. These columns were two-foot-by-two-foot boxes that were at least twenty feet tall. Being naive, I thought they were solid columns and that I had knocked some plaster off the side. As I backed up to observe my damage, I was shocked to see the column was made of sheet rock and I had punched a hole into the column about the size of my fist. Looking closer, I realized this was not nearly as bad as I had anticipated, and I was a little relieved. The hole could easily be repaired, and they were using something like pea gravel as décor to help the column not look so plain. I was sorry that I hit the column and caused some damage. But after inspecting it, I realized this was not nearly as bad as I had once thought it was, and I would make sure the maintenance people were aware of it when I arrived early the next morning.

Early Friday morning, as usual, I ran around picking up doughnuts to sell before school to help raise money for the baseball team. By 8:15 am, I failed to tell maintenance. By about 8:30, the youth pastor at the school came by and asked me if I had hit one of the columns in front of the church. I immediately told him I did and that I meant to tell maintenance when I arrived this morning so they could get it fixed before church on Sunday. He then asked me if I had told anyone at the church, and I said, "no," as I did not think it was a big deal. At this point, he told me the founder had seen the damage and was very upset. The founder had instructed that I park the golf cart outside of his office doors and give him the keys.

I used that golf cart to drag the field for practice, so unless he had a better plan, I wasn't going to give him the keys. We'd just have to see how it played out.

I walked over to see if they had fixed the hole in the column and sure enough, it had already been fixed. I was shocked and impressed at how quickly they gotten the repair done. Also, while I was over there, I noticed there were some big, four-foot-tall concrete poles in front of the other columns that lined the covered, drop-off area. Curious about why we had those poles, I started asking around. Finally, I came across someone that knew the story, and they told me the following.

A few years back, the wife of the children's pastor wife had pulled up into the covered, drop-off area and by mistake had hit one of those columns, causing significant damage. As a result, they had built those smaller pillars to keep people from being able to hit the larger columns again.

Hmm . . . . That was interesting!

I went along with my day and didn't think much about it. The founder had already seen the hole and had it fixed, so it's not like I needed to notify anyone. When I saw him again, I would just explain what happened. When I played it back in my mind, it sounded so simple and easy.

The day progressed as normal, with lunchtime approaching quickly. As I entered the lunchroom, I spotted the founder eating lunch with the high school principal and the headmaster of the school. I thought, *This was going to be interesting*. I said, "Hello men." The founder jumped up to address me and, anticipating what was coming next, the principal grabbed us and hurried us both into his office across from the lunchroom.

He was trying to avoid a full-blown argument in the lunchroom, in front of the entire student body. I will have to be honest with you when I say my *TP blood* (translation: white trash blood) was boiling in my body at this moment, and that may be an understatement. However, I had been anticipating this moment, and I was ready for the founder.

I was the first one to enter his office, and I turned and said, "Please let me say a couple of things and you can then say anything you want."

He gave me the go-ahead. I said, "Doc, I want to say two things. One, I understand you want me to park the golf cart outside your office and give you the keys, because you believe that I was being careless with it and made a hole in one of the columns. Is that correct?"

He confirmed.

I asked him if he took the the keys from the wife of the children's minister and parked her minivan outside his office when she had her accident.

The other men in the office were trying not to laugh out loud. So, I thought this was going better than I thought and maybe I had a legit argument.

I continued. "Secondly, on Wednesday you talked about Matthew 18:21-35, about how the servant owed the king a debt and the king forgave him of the debt and basically told him to learn a lesson about grace and forgiveness. Only to have that very servant, when put in the same situation (two men owed him money and he threw them in jail), did not show the same grace and forgiveness to his own servants. Am I correct in my interpretation of what the parable is saying?"

He confirmed.

"Well, Doc, this is where we have a problem. In the fall, you had an idea that you were going to expand the school and knocked down a $5,000 dugout, and you are yet to rebuild it. Then, by accident, I put a $100 hole in the sheet-rock pillars in front of the sanctuary, and you want me to park the golf cart we use for multiple purposes for the baseball team because you are mad. I do not see any difference in the parable you shared and what has happened in real life. I have not said one word about the dugout, even though we have sat in lawn chairs during a couple of scrimmages (looking like fools) in hopes that you are going to do what you said you would do five months ago. When I made a $100 mistake that paled in comparison to the wrong you have committed against the baseball team, you threatened me and were beside yourself with anger."

He confirmed I had said nothing wrong and did not need to park the golf cart outside his office. I was dismissed to leave the office. Everything was fine. Or so I thought.

At that point, I left the meeting, grabbed lunch, and prepared for baseball practice like I would any other day, never realizing a storm was brewing. I did what I had been taught to do all my life and that was to stand up for myself if I thought I was correct. Do not be disrespectful, but be honest and fair, if I believed I had been wronged or had a legitimate argument.

The next morning, as I arrived an hour early for our Saturday practice to make sure the field was ready and everything was in order, I was shocked to see the founder walking around outside the baseball field. As I walked up to the field, I could see that he had a tape measure and was doing some figuring. He was trying to figure out how he could rectify the wrong he had done. Naturally, I asked him if I could help, and he flatly refused and said he could figure it out. Being a little naïve about grudges, I was shocked he was still a little stand-offish. But I didn't let it bother me and got ready for practice, never thinking any more about it.

Sunday rolled around and, of course, we all attended the church, as usual. As I arrived, I ran into the headmaster and naturally, I asked him how the founder was doing. Much to my surprise, I was informed he was still steaming about how I talked to him on Friday, thinking I was completely disrespectful of his position. I thought I had used his own words and spoken the truth to him. It didn't seem like my problem; it sounded like his. With that, I walked off and went to sit down. Again, not thinking much about what happened, I had no idea a Cat 5 hurricane was coming my way.

The next morning, I did my normal routine, picked up doughnuts, sold them in the cafeteria and went to first period. First period started at 8:15, and I was taking roll when the high school principal walked into the gym and asked to talk to me.

He began to explain to me that he the founder was very put off by my disrespectful tone. He communicated that if I did not go over and apologize to him for my actions and behavior then I no longer had a job.

Not believing what I had just heard, I said, "Let me save you the trouble of firing me. Because if that's the case, then I quit."

"Now coach, just stop for a minute and think about it."

I said, "Think about it. What are you talking about? Everything I said to him was the truth. He had spoken to us about the servant owing the King and not forgiving his servants when the same thing happened to him. He was judged and thrown into jail. That is exactly what he did with the dugout and me making that hole. He was downplaying what he had done wrong and maximizing what I had done. That's not right. If that is how he works, then I am done."

This conversation went on for another 30 mins. At this point, they brought in my best friend and coaching buddy at the school and asked him to talk to me. Phil told me that he completely understood, but none of that was going to change the founder's mind. The biggest point he helped me realize was that the baseball players were going to be without a head coach right before the season started. The players would become collateral damage in this entire ordeal. They didn't even have a dog in the fight, and this would ruin their season; one with a ton of promise. At this point, I started crying. These were not the kind of tears I shed for Brennan McCool; they were tears of rage! I was so angry.

In my office, I just sat and stewed over this situation. Everything I stood for, that I believed in, was on the line. Do right, be honest, and when you are wrong, apologize and be accountable. All those things resonated in my soul, and I was about to lie to myself, and compromise my fundamental core beliefs. To make it even more hypocritical, I was being asked to lie to the head pastor of the church. A church I attended and the place of my employment. A place where he was the leader. All of this so that he could believe he put me in my place, and I got to keep my job!!

Every time I thought of it, I clenched my fists with rage and tears would stream down my face! At about 9:45, the principal walked back over to get me, like I had asked him to. Knowing myself is half the battle, and I learned a long time back that if you are going to have a meeting that can become contentious, then you need to have a witness, or it becomes your word against theirs. I knew I needed to stay under control

As we walked to the church offices off the wing of the sanctuary, I could feel my blood pressure begin to rise. I just kept telling myself to say as little as possible to limit the exposure of attack and conflict. We walked in and I quickly told him that I was sorry and did not mean to come off disrespectful in the conversation that had taken place the previous Friday. To be completely honest, I felt like I blacked out (not really), but I don't think I heard another word he said. I went over, swallowed my pride, and did what was best for the baseball team and those players. But at no point did I do what I thought was best for Greg Vandagriff!

I wanted nothing more than to drag him outside and beat him like a rented mule! Not my proudest moment, but it's how I felt. He was a smug old man who felt self-righteous and made everyone around him feel inferior. It infuriated me, but I did my part and left the office. My job was intact, and he was going to replace the dugout within the next week. As I left, I felt sorry for the school administration and the place I worked. I had just learned that as long as I told the leader of a church and school what he wanted to hear, I could keep my job. It really was a sad day. It was the last day I truly worked there, although I did not leave till a year or so later. Mentally, I had checked out and was already looking for a better opportunity because this was not someone I wanted to work for, ever again. The whole situation was regrettable, but I learned a lot.

THE PATCH

The letter jacket patch I earned through this experience was **#1**, which stands for **the Number 1 rule for life**: life is not fair. On the *Trailer Park White Trash jacket*, this patch can represent anger, bitterness, and the other negative things that happen when you don't handle this rule with the correct perspective. Spending time trying to rationalize things that happen to you and trying to justify whether they make sense or not is a complete waste of time. In a morally and ethically bankrupt world in which people in control often work to ensure their needs are met first, the needs of others are not always a priority. This truth often leads to the lament, "life is not fair." Because it's not. If you know that going in, it can save you a lot of unnecessary wasted time and energy, as you realize that very seldom will things just go your way.

On a positive note, this patch looks better on my *Dad Legends* jacket. I don't have to respond to even the saddest example of this truth with a horrible perspective. I can see beyond the moment.

I have shared *Rules for Life* with my players for years. Rule Number 1: Life is not fair. Ever. I learned that lesson my fourth year of teaching and coaching, but it helped me understand that when you are the leader, you sometimes must make decisions that are best for the whole but not best for the individual. I was the leader, and I was responsible to the young men on the team. If I were to walk in there and tell them that I stood up for myself and as a result I was fired, those kids would say, "Coach, I understand." But when the rubber met the road, they would not care if I was right and got fired. They would have been happier if I apologized, and they got to keep their coach.

The principle to remember here is

Rule Number 1 for life: life is not fair, but don't let that hold you back!

Huddle Up

I am going to be honest when I tell you that learning this rule may be what separates the winners from the losers. This truth is never going away, and your ability to suck it up and be tough for your family will many times make or break your relationship with your wife and your ability to lead your family. According to what profession you are in, you may experience the fact that life is not fair more than others. It does not mean you take the doormat approach to life, but it does mean you may need to weigh putting someone in their place against you keeping your job. In every profession, you will have to do things you do not like, and there are times you may have to work with people you do not get along with. I believe when you are caught in those situations, it's best to keep your job and stable income, but be actively looking for another job or even consider changing your current career.

I've learned that sometimes, as a dad, you must make decisions that are best for your family, especially your kids, even if they're not the best decisions for you, individually. I used to love to play golf, but once we decided to have a family, I could no longer justify those five or more hours a day playing a round of golf. (I know what you golf advocate cry babies are saying: "It takes you five hours to play golf?" No, it does not. But I do have to drive to the course and get ready, pay for my tee times, etc. All of that equals five-plus hours, I promise.) For me, golf is a game I can play when I'm older and the kids are long gone. It really was an easy decision. My choice and mine only. I enjoy playing individual sports, so, to scratch that itch, I had to find other things that were not as time-consuming to play. It was the exact right decision at the right time, and I've never regretted it.

Life is not fair. The quicker you accept this, the better off you will be. But you will be even better off again when you don't let it hold you back.

There are liars, cheaters, and unethical people in the world; don't be shocked when they lie to you, cheat you, or treat you unfairly. But don't be mistaken that you must lie, cheat, and treat others unfairly in return. The truth is, you can choose to wear the *Dad Legends* jacket and respond in a way that can actually still bless and help others, even in the middle of a tough situation.

You need to provide a strong example for your spouse and children.

CHAPTER 8

I CAN'T DRIVE 55

It had been a long time since I had seen Randy, one of my best childhood friends. He was that friend who accepted me for who I was without any reservations or prejudgments. So, when he called and asked if he could stay with me for a couple days while he was in town attending a sales meeting, how could I say no?

The evening started like most any other afternoon that may lead to a little drinking and fun. However, there were a couple of exceptions. It was a Sunday, and it was Valentine's Day. However, we had both just cleared waivers (been dumped by our girlfriends) and were partially licking our wounds and partially pissed. It had the makings of a perfect storm.

We headed downtown, in my brand-new red Corvette (was I screaming for attention or what?). We hit a few spots in Atlanta, but not too many. The plan was to be home fairly early, somewhere between 10 p.m. and midnight, as we both had work the next morning. That was a pretty big deal as I had just been named the new head coach of the worst school in the county. We needed an uneventful night. Well, that was the plan anyway.

We cruised downtown, visited a few establishments and had a few beers. I stopped at two or three beers, but Randy was a little more aggressive and had ten or twelve. I was fine with it; I was driving and those few beers over a three- or four-hour period would not affect me at all.

At about 10 p.m., we looked at each other and decided it was a good time to hit the road, and we settled up with bartender and headed out.

Sammy Hagar wrote a song in the '80s called *I Can't Drive 55*, and he talked about how he liked to drive fast. Evidently, I did too. I had only received a few "fast driving awards" during my driving career, but things were about to change. We headed home, playing the tunes pretty loud in the car. Then, it happened. A black Corvette pulled up next to me and started punching his speed and falling back. He was basically asking me if I wanted to race. Well, of course! Here we go!

Let's review the elements of this perfect storm:

1. Valentine's Day and I am single, which translated to being a little irritated and pissed.
2. Hanging with a buddy I had not seen in a while, and we bring out the "daredevils" in one another.
3. Driving a new Corvette (they don't make those things to go slow, in case you did not know)
4. Natural Competitor: I just got challenged, so now I've got to go get that win.

Back to the action. The black Corvette pulled up and basically called me out to race. My buddy gave me a "let's go" then rolled down his window to flip the black Corvette a bird. I was trying to get Randy back into the car as we took off.

The black Corvette and I were weaving in and out of traffic, rolling up I-75 at about 110 mph. It really had not gotten dangerous at this time. We were racing but traffic was light (as most couples and lovers were home on Valentine's; only the rejects and heartbroken fools were out). We got the lead after a few miles and continued up to the I-285 interchange, at which point I backed off. I didn't want to press my luck, and I believed we were the winners already. However, the *Corvette Villain* I was racing against got really aggressive. He got on my tailgate and started swerving towards us, wanting to race again. I am not sure what happened next except that something snapped inside me, and I decided it was enough. I looked over at Randy and said, "Hold on, its about to get real," as I dropped the transmission back into fourth and stomped the gas. I had made a personal decision that I was about to find out how fast this car could go.

As I stomped the gas and shot over to the inside lane, we started screaming up the north-bound lanes. The odometer was racing 100, 110, 120. I was trying to see where the soon-to-be two-time loser was but I really couldn't take my eyes off the windshield, as we were barreling down on other vehicles. I was having to swerve into the emergency portion of the inside lane to avoid hitting unsuspecting drivers. Not seeing the menace in my rearview mirror, I pressed forward, and the odometer climbed to 130, then 140. We had traveled five or six miles by this time, and I was still pressing the limits 144, 145, 146, 147… that was the last time I even peeked at the odometer as people in front of us did not have a chance to react as we were flying by them. As we capped the next small ridge, I thought I saw blue lights as far back in the rearview mirror as I could see. Reality came crashing down on me as those blue lights became a new reality.

I was no longer worried about winning, but rather about surviving the next few minutes. We had just passed the 120-loop in Marietta and were headed towards Barrett Parkway when our joy ride home was interrupted. I am not sure what happened to the black Corvette demon. It was as if he just "poof" disappeared. And my buddy began to panic and stress about the "Man" closing in on us. Making some quick calculations and analyzing this situation, I decided to shoot across five lanes of traffic and hit the Canton Highway exit. I figured I could get off the interstate, pull into a nearby neighborhood, let things calm down and a few hours later go home. I knew I was coming across another hill and if I hit it right, the cop would never see me exit the interstate, and we could be home free.

As I was exiting, I never saw the cop make the hill and just knew that we were about to get lucky and make it. Speeding off the curved exit and preparing to slow down to merge into to traffic, I was dumbfounded when four cop cars had the intersection blocked off waiting for me. Running out of viable options, I pulled that little red Corvette over next to the curb. As the cops came running to my car, I cracked my electronic window about three inches and politely slid my license out the window and waited for them to arrive. As the first cop got to the window, I looked up at him and said, "Is there a problem, Officer?" Let's just say he could not get me out of the car and get the cuffs on me fast enough. They promptly took me to the back of the cop car and placed me inside.

Well, these were uncharted waters I was swimming in. I had never been in the back of a cop car and can only remember driving by and wondering what those "idiots" had done to get arrested. Now, here I was—one of those idiots! It seemed like I had been sitting there for what felt like an eternity when they came and got me out of the car. Standing outside the car now, they began to tell me all the "driving awards" (tickets) I had earned was about to receive.

The tickets were as follows:

Speeding—(I thought, "Well, that's true.") I asked what they had me clocked at and they replied, "110." Dropping my head, I responded with "Yes Sir." I was not sure if 147 was worse but I knew it could not be better.

Reckless Driving—(No Response) True as charged.

Racing – Again, guilty as charged.

Following too close—Now here is where I had a problem. (Naturally, I was only thinking all of these supplemental thoughts to myself. To the cops, I was nice and quiet.) When I heard this charge, I thought, *How can I get a 'following too close' ticket when I was in the lead and when approaching the other cars, I was past them so fast, I did not even have time to follow them?* I wanted to draw the line with this ticket. The other three were completely accurate but this one was, in football terms, just piling on.

They informed me that my car would be impounded, and I was being taken to jail. I asked them about Randy, and they told me they would call him a cab (this is way before Uber). They took me over to Randy who was lying on the side of the curb passed out. I could not help but laugh while wishing I could pass out and wake up later from this nightmare I had willfully decided to create! I did my best to wake Randy up enough so that he could get home. As I was talking to him, the cab driver pulled up. Realizing there was no way Randy would remember my address, I paid the cab driver and told him where to take him. Then, it was back to the traveling jail cell for me.

What seemed like an eternity was actually only a ten- to

fifteen-minute ride to the county jail. They photographed and fingerprinted me and placed me into a holding cell with another "award winner." Before entering I was able to call my roommate and ask him to come and get me. It was only about 11:30 p.m. at this time, and my buddy said he would be there as soon as he could.

During the next few minutes, that felt like hours, I had plenty of time to reflect on my split-second decision that had potentially changed my life forever. At this time, I was about 29 years old, and my dad had been in the federal penitentiary for the past five years. A flood of emotions came pouring over me as I began to think about all of the people who had told me I would never amount to anything. My mind began to list all the things they had said:

Trailer Trash
Not going to amount to anything.
Look at your parents – you will never be anything.
You don't have a chance due to how you grew up.

I thought of the people I had let down who had poured so much into my life, from my mother to all the coaches who had encouraged me to dare to be better than my environment. I thought of the mentors who had spoken life to me and the FCA Leaders and other Christian friends who helped me seek a better path. I had thrown all of this down the toilet in a matter of minutes. That single moment of realization seemed endless.

As I sat there wallowing in my own self-pity, I started praying, negotiating, or pleading for God to help me, one more time! I remembered so many times God had been so good to me. And here I sat, begging for His mercy, His forgiveness, and His favor. I needed the one thing He promises that cannot be earned and that I did not deserve. His Grace. I made a promise to God. I laid out my part, telling God that if He would help me through this time of insanity that I would never look back and never embarrass Him again. I prayed that prayer and trusted God would show up – why would I believe anything else? He had consistently shown up in my life, saving me from my own destruction and guiding me when I was blind. I had no reason to believe this would not occur again, not because of anything special about me. But because of His character.

My roommate came through for me, paid the bail and got me out of jail. Of course, at that point, we had to go get my car out of the impound yard. The whole thing felt like throwing money in an empty hole. But eventually, we made it home. The next morning, I sat in my bed and began to attack my problem. I reached out to a few friends to find an attorney that would represent me, as I was in trouble. The four tickets I had received equaled enough points that, according to our state statutes, I would lose my license unless I could find an answer. A friend suggested an attorney who liked to help coaches, and I gave him a ring. Over the next few minutes, we laid out a plan, and I went to work on my part.

I had about three months before the court case, but I wanted to be prepared to show the eventual judge that I had learned my lesson. One of the first things I was encouraged to do was attend defensive driving school. No problem. I signed up immediately and attended the class. Holy cow, what a room of degenerates. I sat by myself, kept my head down and bided my time, hoping I did not get stabbed or high while I was there.

Alright, first assignment completed. I had my own ideas about some things I could do to help myself as well. As I pulled into the Nissan Dealership and parked my 'Vette behind their 300Z, a salesman quickly walked out to greet me. As he walked up asking me if I was looking to trade in my car, I said "As a matter of fact, I am." Obviously, he thought I as going to go for the 300, but I kept walking right past it, with my eyes locked onto one of their small Nissan trucks. The salesman could not believe his ears when he heard me ask about the '97 pickup truck. I told him that I needed to purchase something that felt like it was going to blow-up when it got to 65 mph, and he said, "Well, you have chosen the right vehicle."

During the time between my "High Speed Racer" fiasco to my court date, I had been named the head football coach to one of the local high schools. I had written a manual about how important character was in schools, written a character education program and done some other work to show the presiding judge that I had truly learned my lesson.

Meeting my attorney outside the court room, I was hopeful that one or two of the charges would be reduced and I would keep my license. I handed him all the proof of the things I had done to right my wrong and he said he would take it from there.

My case number was called, and we approached the bench. My attorney walked over and talked to the representing D.A., pointed at me, and said a few things. Then they both walked up to the judge. A few more conversations were had, and the judge looked at me then back at them. I just sat there while my fate was being decided. The judge then looks at me and asks me to approach the bench. One of the interesting things about this entire thing was that the judge was talking in a very low voice, and it appeared they were being a little discreet (for which I was thankful). As I approached the bench, the judge looked at me and said, "Will you plead guilty to a contest of speed? If so, I will drop all the charges against you, and you will be free to go." I could not believe my ears. I could not say "Yes Sir" fast enough and my attorney and I walked out.

As we got outside, I turned to my representative and asked him how much I owed him for all the work. He just smiled and said "Don't worry about it. All you do for kids and our community; I am more than glad to be able to pay you back some." I was flabbergasted! I could not believe what I had heard. I said, "Honestly, how much money did you just save me?" He smiled and said, "About $1,500." I hugged him and felt like I was skipping to "Black Beauty," the black Nissan pick-up truck that I was now driving.

God had done it again. Now it was my turn to keep my promise to Him.

I have many stories and experiences, but I do not believe any of them changed my life more than this one. As the country music song goes, "I was old enough to know better, but I was still too young to care." It had never been truer. The morning after this event, the guilt (for my failure to God) and personal humiliation changed me forever. I am grateful for all the favor that was shown to me and never wanted to place myself in a situation like this again.

I still own the Nissan. It sits in my driveway as a constant reminder: One quick impulsive decision could cost me everything. Life is that short. Plain and simple, impulsive decisions wreck families and ruin lives!

The Patch

The letter jacket patch I earned through this experience was a **G for grace**. This is a patch I needed on my *Trailer Park White Trash* letter jacket for sure. But it wasn't only then. The G still stands for grace on the *Dad Legends* jacket as well. Why? Because I still need His grace. And I am still so thankful for it!

A biblical definition for grace is, *God's favor upon those who have broken His laws and sinned against Him.* I am not sure there is a better word to sum up how I felt after the judge basically threw out all the tickets and did away with the points I had earned that were going to affect my driver's license and insurance. Not to mention the embarrassment that I could have received at the school I was now serving as the head football coach. I had been trying to downplay this for months, but in essence, this had the potential to cost me my job if some sort of miracle did not take place. I truly needed something I did not deserve and that was grace.

God granting me His favor in this situation taught me a ton about giving grace to the players I coached. As a matter of fact, one of the first "rules to coach by" that the coaches at Kell High School and myself came up with was this: If in doubt when disciplining a player, we would give grace, if at all possible. Young men (and evidently older men) make mistakes at times and do some stupid things. When you give another person grace, it can be life changing.

This is the lesson I wanted to pass forward to my children and to the young men who were placed under my tutelage. I believe it's important to learn lessons from our mistakes. But you can also learn when there is true remorse in your heart and grace has been granted to you.

Sitting in that jail cell, I kept thinking about how the split-second decision to find out how fast that Corvette could go had placed my entire life in peril. I was embarrassed. I wanted to go back to that very moment and change it. I thought back to that very first Superman movie where Christopher Reeve flew around the world to go back in time and save Lois Lane. I wanted to do this with my own life and undo that horrible decision. However, I was going to have to sit right there in jail and think about my cocaine-dealing father who was sitting in jail in another state just like his convict son. I was embarrassed. This was not the person God had created me to be, and I had made a mockery of His gifts for me. God had allowed me to walk through so many learning opportunities. He had spared me from all kinds of crime, drugs and alcohol that had always been around me. And how did I thank Him? By making an absolutely selfish and stupid decision. He had just placed me in front of seventy-five (mostly fatherless) young men to be their head coach. And what had I done to repay His favor? I had tried to throw it all away. Then, when I needed it most, God stood up, looked down into that court room, and whispered into the ear of the judge, "Let's show this young man grace." From that moment, my life has changed forever!

Grace can change your life! That's exactly what happened to me. On the verge of losing everything I had worked for, God said, "He is one of mine and I am choosing to forgive him even though he has done absolutely nothing to deserve it." Grace cannot be bought. It cannot be bartered for. It is given to someone who does not deserve it! That was me, and I thank God for looking down and gifting me grace. One more time!

The last principle I want to share with dads is this one, and it has the power to be life altering.

Grace when shared at precisely the right moment can be a life-changing event.

Huddle Up

It is so hard to teach a child what grace truly is until they experience it. When you give your child grace, you are hoping they will realize how fortunate they are to receive favor and forgiveness without consequences. However, then too, they may not realize what it means. They may just celebrate that they didn't get into trouble. Regardless, please remember that your job is to teach them how powerful grace can be, but it's their job to realize that it is an underserved gift given without strings attached.

I believe discipline is a big part of raising your children. These words are almost considered taboo in today's society, but I still believe there has to be some threat of consequences when a child starts to do something they know they shouldn't do. Here's an example. When my son, Brock, was a child, I wanted his brain to associate certain decisions with certain consequences. For instance, I hoped something like this would be his internal dialogue if he had a dust-up with his sister:

"My 6-year-old sister has made me mad, and I am going to hit her. Oh wait, if I do that my dad has told me it results in a 'belt' spanking, no questions asked. Because we never lay our hands on a female, regardless of the reason."

I realize some of you who are between 20 and 30 just about threw this book across the room because you are so offended. Hang in there, as I am twice your age, and corporal punishment was a rite of passage when I was a kid. I am more than sure the threat of getting spanked with a switch from my grandmother kept me from getting too rough with my older sister.

Having said this about discipline, I also believe there are times when your child shows true remorse, and you throw them a lifeline and give them grace. We can trust God to lead us as we lead our children. Isn't that a beautiful thought in itself? My Father gives me grace. How can I not, in turn, share grace with others, especially my children. Rather than just proving a point, it can change lives.

Conclusion

It has taken me years to come up with a way to share these stories so maybe they could benefit someone besides myself. As I examined my heart and searched my mind for the reason why I had such a burden to share them, the one answer that kept coming back to me was this: I wanted to help other dads who felt like they did not have an example to follow but still yearned to be a good dad. That is my entire purpose in writing this book. I hope some other young man will get his hands on this book, and it will give him the courage to do the best job he can in a broken world full of bad examples. Or I hope that this book will inspire a dad who has been beating himself up about feeling ill prepared to be a dad. I hope it can help him realize that his children do not want a perfect dad, they just want a present one!

Our entire country would be a better place if the dads in the world spent more time being responsible for the children they have helped bring into the world. The stats presented a little later below point out how many homes are falling apart, and how many children are suffering, due to financial hardship or morally bankrupt environments without the dad being present in the home. Almost always the mom is doing her job, but it's time for men to stand up, raise their hands, and say they are willing to accept their role within the home. We need men who have a burning desire to be part of the answer in this world. It's time for them to stop worrying about how prepared they are and realize that most children and wives want to know they are loved first. The rest will usually take care of itself.

We all have experiences that shape our decision-making. Your life may not have been as "entertaining" as mine or it may have been two times more sensational. I have no idea, but I do know that all of us make choices and decisions based upon our life experiences. I hope you will join me in helping your children learn how to be good adults who will also choose to be part of the answer. Also, once your children start their adulthood years, I hope that you will look around your own community and choose to help those around you learn how to be good dads as well. I hope that you will choose to be a mentor to other young men.

I know I have been pushing men to step up, but don't just take my word for it. Here are the latest statistics about homes where the dad is absent, as provided by the America First Policy Institute (https://americafirstpolicy.com/issues/issue-brief-fatherlessness-and-its-effects-on-american-society).

- **Poverty**: Fatherless families are four times more likely to live in poverty than families with married couples.
- **Mental health**: Children from fatherless homes may have lower self-esteem, anxiety, social withdrawal, and depression. They may also be at a higher risk of suicide and other forms of self-harm.
- **Behavioral disorders**: According to the Center for Disease Control, 85 percent of children who exhibit

behavioral disorders come from fatherless homes.

- **Drug and alcohol abuse**: The U.S. Department of Health and Human Services says that fatherless children are at a higher risk of drug and alcohol abuse.
- **Education**: 71 percent of high school dropouts come from fatherless homes.
- **Homelessness**: 90 percent of homeless and runaway children come from fatherless homes.
- **Criminal justice**: 85 percent of youths in prison come from fatherless homes, and 80 percent of rapists motivated by displaced anger come from fatherless homes.

As you can clearly see, not having a dad is catastrophic for children. God never intended for fathers to abandon their children. We need to step up and be accountable to those around us. I know what you are thinking, "I am just one person." But it all starts with one person being willing to say, "I want to be part of the answer." Then he challenges his friend, and the problem begins to get smaller.

Unfortunately, men are often not doing their part. In our broken world, one surefire way to address the broken home issue is for the dad to do his part inside the home. Any man who reads this book and has a desire for his home to be changed needs to realize it happens one day at a time. If you are going to change your "broken family tree" then it starts with the dad modeling the behavior he needs his children to have.

Joining the *Dad Legends* team should be a desire of every man in the country. Having your children look back on their childhood memories with smiles on their faces is a worthy aspiration. Being a *Dad Legend* does not mean you have to jump over buildings with a single bound, but it does mean you have to be present when your child needs you in the middle of the night. Being any kind of legend takes being present and consistent in their lives.

My prayer for you is that you are inspired and encouraged to be part of the answer in this equation. I pray that you have the burning desire to inspire your own children to be the best they can. Lastly, I pray that you will inspire other dads around you to catch the fever and inspire them to join the team!

Let's Go—"Dad Legends" on three!

One, two, three . . . *Dad Legends!*

OUR CODE

Eight Principles we (The Dad Legends) choose to use to help us Guide our Lives

1. Your current circumstances do not determine your future destination.
2. To be a dad every child wants to be proud of, you must become a man worth following.
3. In life, you need to control the controllables and refuse to beat yourself up over things out of your control.
4. It's imperative that you have a plan for your life and that you plan your work and work your plan.
5. Embrace the *Dirt Road of Life* Philosophy: Stand up, dust your pants off, and get busy walking towards your goals.
6. Dad, once you start your own team, you accept the responsibilities of being the Owner, CFO, and Head Coach.
7. Rule Number 1 for Life: Life is not fair, do not ever forget it!
8. Grace, when shared at precisely the right moment, can be a life-changing event.

Do You want to be a Legend?

There are many different types of legends in this world. There are good ones and bad ones. There are stories of larger-than-life people who supposedly did something astounding, but the real legends are the ones who wake up every day and get busy making a difference in their kids' lives. The legends I want to inspire are the ones who are not looking to be patted on the back but would rather spend their time empowering the next generation to pass the torch!

A *Dad Legend* is a man who does not make excuses for his lack of preparation but rather gets busy finding a way to succeed. I believe children would gladly have less of any worldly thing if that meant they got to spend more quality time with their dads.

Joining the *Dad Legends* team means that you are willing to help other dads and be there for children when their fathers are not around. It is not their fault that their fathers have not chosen to take the *Dirt Road Philosophy* of life. It is not their fault that their friends' fathers have not joined a team that simply wants more out of life.

A willingness to be a member of the *Dad Legends* team includes an acknowledgment that you want to be different from the other fathers.

I want you to take a moment and finish this little exercise with me. . .and if you truly mean what you are about to say, I want you to sign and date the following contract to commemorate the moment you committed to joining the team. I realize it's not for everyone. And there are plenty of excuse-making, sorry fathers in the world. I just hope you are not one of them!

At this time, I want you to raise your right hand. No, really. Raise your right hand and repeat after me.

- I realize that to be a *Dad Legend*, I must give a legendary effort.
- I accept the financial responsibility for my family's needs.
- I acknowledge that I will have setbacks and failures, but those moments will not define my life.
- I am going to embrace the *Dirt Road Philosophy* of life and with that, I am going to stand up, dust off my pants, and get busy.
- I realize that, as a *Dad Legend,* I am not only responsible for my children, but I am willing to help their friends as well.
- I refuse to forget Rule Number 1—Life is not fair and every day I complain about it robs me of a day I can get better.
- I will never forget that grace is the greatest gift given to us. It starts with Jesus giving us grace first.

Signature _____

Date ____/____/____

Acknowledgements

For many years people have encouraged me to tell my story. They would say, wow, it's amazing you are able to function like you do or be successful. The issue was I never knew how to wrap it up and have it be worthwhile for others to read. I want to thank Gabe Norris for encouraging me to put my story on paper and get it out there. I want to thank Dawn Sherrill-Porter, my editor, for taking my "Coach Speak" and putting it into words that flowed and made sense but never allowed my voice to not be heard. I want to thank my publisher, Mike Parker of WordCrafts Press, for helping fledgling authors like myself have a place to dream and avenue to get our stories out there for others to hear.

Lastly, I am thankful for all of the men that poured their life into mine during my early years. I am sure there are some I will miss but none were more instrumental than Wayne Norfleet (my College AD) and Larry Kerr (my HS FB Coach). Also, I want to thank my wife, Kelly and my children, Brock, Anna, and Audrey for allowing me to be part of your lives and riding along with me. And, I want to apologize to all of those people I mistreated and did wrong along the way due to my ignorance or stupidity. I hope you will accept my apology and hope to see you on the other side.

ABOUT THE AUTHOR

Greg Vandagriff grew up in an abnormally dysfunctional home. "We grew up in a trailer park without sufficient finances," he explains. "My mother married four times, and my father figures were poor examples. My biological father spent 20 years in federal penitentiary, the second man my mother married was an alcoholic, the third one placed a gun to his head and pulled the trigger. By the time the fourth one came to live with my mom, I was gone."

Fortunately, during his formative years, Greg spent a great deal of time with his grandmother who was a devoted Christian who was faithful to her Baptist church. She made sure her grandchildren attended church when they came for a visit. And Greg credits his high school football coach as the stabilizing force in my life at the time. "More than anyone else, he helped me understand what walking with Christ looked like," he muses.

Greg has since gone on to a stellar 35-yeat career as a football coach. But he insists at this point in his life the most important this is sharing more about Jesus and what God has done for his family.